CONTENTS

Chapter 5

Who Runs the Pension Fund?   55

Chapter 6

Cost to Manage the Fund   69

Chapter 7

A Little Piece of the Action   83

Chapter 11

The Role of Retirees   161

Chapter 12

The Proper Role of Government   169

Chapter 13

In Summary   181

CHAPTER 1

Introduction

Ivan Boesky.

That name conjures up memories of insider trading scandals that rocked the securities business. The remarkable thing is so many people thought this conduct was just a part of "doing business." As Michael Douglas put it in his role as an unethical, high-flying financier in the 1987 movie, *Wall Street:* "Greed is good."

Greed and wrongdoing did not stop at the securities firms, however, and it certainly did not end with the 1980s. The opportunity for making a few extra bucks has spread to that seeming bastion of conservatism, the corporate pension fund. Billions of dollars of corporate pension fund assets, which are intended to secure the retirement promise of millions of people can be the target of self-serving company employees who are out to enrich themselves. These company employees, who range from senior executives to those who work in the pension fund, can use very sophisticated tricks to get what they want. And pension plan participants will not be any the wiser as to what really went on, until it is too late.

Don't think that just because a pension fund was safe in the past it will be secure in the future. These are the underlying realities:

1. The new culture of the disposable employee has diminished loyalties and trust within corporations. This harsher business environment can create an atmosphere where fraud and wrongdoing might flourish.

1

2. Pension fund investment management, consulting, and trading financial instruments are lucrative businesses. There are thousands of firms scrambling for a piece of the action. This creates opportunities for self-serving employees to exploit for their own personal advantage.

3. Conscientious trustees and senior executives who lack pension fund investment "street smarts" might be easily lulled into a false sense of security by clever employees.

4. Senior executives can retaliate against whistle-blowing pension fund employees with relative impunity; knowing this, people will think twice before reporting wrongdoing.

5. New executive compensation packages at many companies could focus senior management's attention on increasing corporate earnings at the expense of the company's pension promise.

6. Some senior executives might believe the pension fund's assets really belong to the company, not to plan participants, and therefore can be used to advance corporate goals.

7. Plan participants are not entitled to any information about their pension fund other than what is required by law — information which is meaningless and incomprehensible to most individuals.

8. "Golden parachutes" may encourage senior executives to proceed with mergers and acquisitions that have a negative impact on the pension promise but result in a huge financial windfall for themselves.

9. If a company is committed to protecting its senior executives it has the money and legal power to frustrate the most diligent of investigators. It is difficult to detect wrongdoing in a pension fund from the outside looking in.

Trustees, who are responsible for overseeing pension fund investments, must address these realities. If they don't, the pension promise for millions of people is at risk. Spending more tax dollars for more government investigators won't solve the problem. It is too easy these days to hide fiduciary misconduct. The effective response is to attack the problem from within the pension fund. The trustee needs to lead the way for change, spurred on by plan participants. The law dictates that all the money in a pension fund is the purview of the plan, and a trustee is obligated, by law, to see that it is properly managed and *solely* in the interest of the plan's participants.

Knowledge of what can really go on is the key. This book gives an inside look at the pension fund industry. Although wrongdoing can occur in many plans, it focuses on defined benefit plans offered by companies. These plans promise a retiree a specific monthly dollar amount at retirement based on a plan participant's age, salary, length of service, and other factors. The pension funds supporting these plans are controlled by company employees. Putting it into perspective, there are approximately 65,000 corporate sponsored defined benefit plans in the United States, covering 41 million people with over $1.4 trillion of pension assets in the plans.

This book describes in detail how company employees can use the assets and resources of the company's pension fund to advance their own careers and personal wealth; how self-interest might become the overriding motivation behind "investment" decisions; and how easy it is to hide these activities from anyone on the outside looking in.

Remember, however, that this is not an exhaustive list of fraud, wrongdoing, and questionable activities in the pension fund industry. There are plenty of opportunities for company employees to use the pension fund as their own personal wealth foundation. When it comes to money, the creativity of greed never ceases to amaze.

Finally, this book is not about finger pointing. It's about change. Examples of fraud, wrongdoing, and questionable activities are only given to provide a foundation for the rationale behind concrete suggestions as to what trustees and plan participants can do to help safeguard pension assets. These recommended changes are not a complete list, nor will implementing these ideas automatically safeguard the thousands of defined benefit corporate pension funds in the United States—but at least these suggestions represent steps in the right direction. Most people who are involved in the pension fund process should welcome them.

The author believes that most pension funds operate under the strict scrutiny of people who take their responsibilities seriously. But even if the vast majority of plans are currently well-managed and the assets of most pension funds are currently secure, why take a chance with the retirement well-being of millions of people? Things change. Senior management and other employees come and go. Priorities get rearranged.

Some very straightforward safeguards need to be put into place, and *now*. That old-fashioned "ounce of prevention" is in order before it is too late. For once, let's correct something before it becomes a disaster.

CHAPTER 2

Principles of Pension Fund Administration

Most people instinctively know their pension fund is important to their retirement well-being, but they don't know why. Either they were never told or they have been confused by the technical terms. This chapter is intended to do something about that. It describes the basics of pension fund administration in a straightforward manner and demonstrates that what goes on in a pension fund can have a major, direct impact on the safety and size of the pension promise.

A PENSION FUND

Sometimes the terms pension *plan* and *pension* fund are used as if they were interchangeable. They are not. A pension plan is just that, a plan. It outlines the retirement income benefits, who is entitled to receive them, when, and who pays for what. On the other hand, a pension fund is where the money resides and from which retirement checks are paid.

One is talk and promises; the other is money and reality.

This is an important distinction. To reinforce it, consider this analogy. Say the parents of a newly born child are concerned about their child's college education, so they devise a plan. They estimate how much it is likely to cost to send their child to college, how much they will pay, and how much their child needs to contribute from summer jobs. Just like a pension plan, this college education plan spells out who is to pay for what, when, and for how long.

Sure, the parents may have entered into their college education plan with good intentions, but things happen. Life does not always work out as we had hoped. Medical bills, loss of a job, or a whole host of other problems can prevent them from keeping their promise. When the time comes 18 or 19 years into the future, the money for college just might not be there.

To make sure it is, most financial consultants will advise the parents to save for this future commitment by putting aside a little cash each month. If the money is invested wisely, the account will grow gradually larger and larger, and when their child starts college the money for tuition will be there. Putting aside a little each month lessens the burden on family finances. The commitment becomes more manageable. Maybe the parents will get lucky and their investments will do so well that, after a while, no more contributions are needed. But chances are they will be prudent and will not "roll the dice" with this money.

Saving for the future is the same idea behind a pension fund. By setting up a pension fund and making contributions into it, the company is "saving" to make good on its retirement promises. It, too, accumulates the contributions it has made and invests the money. If everything goes well, the company employees invest wisely, and the managers are ethical, the money should be in the fund to keep the retirement promises the company has made.

Money in the pension fund provides plan participants with the peace of mind that, come what may, the pension promise will be kept. Plan participants are counting on that promise to be kept over the next 10, 20, 30, 40 or more years. That's a long time. Economies turn down, industries falter and change, senior executives may decide to delay putting money into the pension fund or fiddle with the assumptions, and companies have been known to go bankrupt. Many things can happen in the future that might prevent a company from completely living up to its retirement promises. A pension fund is there to guarantee the promises are kept.

A DYNAMIC PROCESS

A pension fund deals with the pension promise for hundreds or thousands of plan participants, not just one individual as described in the college education fund example. Employees leave the company before retirement age or move up or down in pay; some, sadly, die before they can collect on the retirement promise. A pension fund must cover all these possibilities.

It sounds strange, but a water tower — with its inflows, holding tank, and outflows — is conceptually similar to a pension fund. Surely you have seen these towers. They dot the suburban landscape. Using a water tower as an analogy will help illustrate how a pension fund works.

Consider this. When someone turns on a faucet, the water stored in the tower flows out of the bottom of the tank into pipes and makes its way to the customer. Other customers turn on their faucets, and more water flows out. As the water continues to flow out of the tank, the level of water drops. When it declines a certain amount, a sensing mechanism activities a pump, and more water is pumped in. The water continues to be pumped in until the tank is replenished, then the pump shuts off.

That's fairly straightforward. What may not be realized, however, is that, to some extent, those in charge of supplying this important resource can manage the process. Clearly, many factors are beyond their ability to control, such as people moving away, hot weather, and geological conditions. But the process can be managed. First, consider the demand for water. The village fathers can control this by limiting the number and type of building permits they issue. This, in turn, will control how many people and what types of industry move into the village and that, in turn, will control the demand for water and, hence, the outflow from the tank. So, by controlling building permits the village can control the outflow of water from the tank. Next, consider the supply of water. The village fathers could add additional wells and/or install a bigger pump to increase the amount of water flowing into the tank. Either would increase the amount of water flowing into the tank. Finally, consider the size of the tank itself. If the village fathers made it bigger, it might help the managers to better match the timing of the inflows with the outflows and provide a margin of safety should anything happen to either the well or the pump.

A Pension Fund's Flows

Now think of a pension fund as if it were a water tower (see Figure 2–1). The company puts money into the tank (makes its contributions), where it stays until it flows out to make benefit payments to the

FIGURE   2–1

Overview of Pension Fund Process

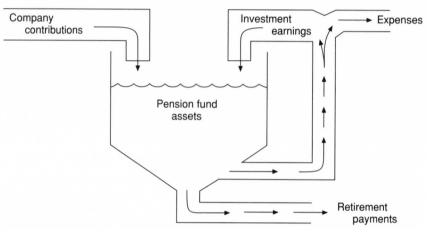

Source: Adapted from C.L. Trowbridge and C.E. Farr, *The Theory and Practice of Pension Funding* (Burr Ridge, IL: Richard D. Irwin, Inc., 1976).

retirees. While the money is in the tank, it gets invested and earns a return, which flows back into the tank increasing (or reducing in the case of investment losses) the amount of money in the tank. In the process, expenses to run the pension fund are paid, reducing the amount of money flowing back into the tank from investments. The level of money in the pension fund is influenced by the dynamic system of inflows from contributions and investment earnings and outflows to make benefit payments and to pay expenses.

If money flows out of the pension fund to make benefit payments faster than it can be replenished from investment earnings or from company contributions, the level of money in the tank goes down. Eventually, the tank will run dry. How fast depends on (1) how much money is in the pension fund to begin with; (2) how fast the money is flowing out; and (3) how fast (if at all) money is being pumped in. While we might not know precisely when, one thing is for certain: The pension fund *will* run out of money if the money flows out faster than it flows in. If not corrected, this situation could have serious consequences for plan participants.

Just like our village fathers in the water tower example, senior executives can, to some extent, manage the process. Clearly, many factors are beyond their ability to control, such as investment market conditions, which would impact investment inflows, or a poor business climate, which would impact a company's financial health and hence its ability to make contributions. Nevertheless, to a large extent the process can be managed.

First, consider the size of the outflow to make benefit payments. A company can control this through changes in its pension plan. For example, assume the company wanted to reduce the size of future outflows from the pension fund. A straightforward way to do so is simply to change the formula used to calculate pension benefits. For example, one element in a defined benefit pension plan formula is an employee's wages. Some companies use the average of the last 5 years for that input to the benefits formula. What happens, though, if instead of using the average of the last 5 years a company decides to use something else — say the average of the last 10 years? By including more years in the averaging calculation, the average wage will go down because, in general, employees earn more later in their careers than earlier. If the average wage used in the benefits formula goes down, that will cause the retirement benefits for employees to go down, and that in turn will reduce the outflow as compared to what it would have been had the changes not been made.

Yet another way to reduce the size of future outflows from a pension fund is to fire older employees. Many retirement formulas use age and the length of service to compute retiree benefit payments. The way some formulas work, the big increases in promised retirement income comes later in an employee's career. By cutting this build-up process short (i.e., firing older workers with longer service records), a company can reduce the retirement income they will receive and that, in turn, will reduce the outflow from the pension fund as compared to what it would have been were the changes not made. Our government thankfully has enacted some antidiscrimination laws that make it harder for companies to fire people just because of their age.

The example of one middle-aged employee who got caught up in a downsizing move illustrates the build-up process:

> Under [the company's] plan I would have been able to collect my full pension after I had 30 years of service, or when I had worked there at least 25 years and reached age 50. I would have been entitled to about $200,000 in a lump-sum pension distribution, 100 percent medical coverage for my wife and I, a life insurance policy worth

more than $100,000 and some other minor benefits. When I was
fired I had an excellent work record . . . But with the day [the com-
pany] set as my termination date (which included a two-year early retirement credit) I was three months short of the 30 years of service
need for a full pension. The company told me I was entitled to
$58,000 and no other benefits.[1]

Any company that can increase turnover within its workforce
will minimize its pension expense as compared to a company that has
a lower level of turnover. This is because most defined benefit pension plans determine the size of benefits based on a formula that
includes two key elements — length of service and salary. Newer employees typically earn less and therefore will receive less. But there's
more to it than that. The build-up of pension income typically accel-
erates with years of service, as the above quote so poignantly illustrates. Just a few months made the difference between a $200,000
payment and one of $58,000. If the build-up process is cut short and
salaries are kept low, with high employee turnover, a corporation can
reduce its pension expense and realize higher short-term corporate
profits, all else being equal. Senior executives, of course, have to
weigh the reduction in pension expense against other factors, such as
productivity and morale, before they decide to implement this strategy and to what degree they will take it.

So senior executives can control to some extent the outflow from
the pension fund via changes in the company's pension plan and
changes in its personnel practices. More and more companies are
learning this, and perhaps pension expense is one of the key inputs to
a downsizing decision.

Now consider the inflows into the pension fund from investments. Investment markets can't be controlled. They are simply too
large. However, senior executives can control how the pension fund's
money is invested and this, in turn, will influence investment returns.
For example, consider two pension funds, one whose management
chose to invest heavily in common stocks 10 years ago and another
which invested heavily in T-bills. Since common stocks outperformed
T-bills over this time frame, the pension fund that invested in common stocks would have had greater inflows from investment returns,
and, as a result, today would be substantially larger than the one that

---

1. "For Middle-Age Workers, a Scary, Non-Linear Story," *Chicago Tribune*, August 1994.

selected T-bills. Now consider the fate of a third pension fund that invested heavily in real estate in the mid-1980s — right at the top of the real estate market. Today that fund is probably suffering huge losses. For example, one pension fund was reported to have written down its real estate holdings by a whopping $550 million.

Investment choices count, but returns should not be separated from risk. While over the past 10 years T-bills provided less return than stocks, the volatility in that return was substantially less. (More about this risk/return trade-off concept in the next chapter.) The point here is that the size of the inflow into the pension fund tank from investment returns is influenced by the investments senior executives make with the pension fund's assets.

Inflows from company contributions can also be controlled. However, before that can be explained, another element needs to be introduced — pension liabilities.

PENSION LIABILITIES

How much money a company owes to its pension plan participants in order to live up to its retirement promises is not an easy question to answer. It depends on many assumptions. This lack of certainty as to an answer frustrates people.

When a company sets up a defined benefit pension plan it is faced with many unknowns. For example, how many employees will stick around long enough to qualify for a pension? How many will opt for early retirement? How much will an employee earn during his or her career? How long will a retiree live? How many employees will die before retiring? How many will opt for surviving spouse retirement benefits? All of this input, and more, enters into the determination of how much a company owes its plan participants.

In addition, the magnitude of these inputs is constantly changing. The company is still in business; it is a going concern, and tomorrow or next year salaries will change, new people will be hired, others will be let go, and pension benefits could be changed. So how much a company owes in order to make good on its promises will vary with time.

One method (and there are others) to simplify the estimation process is to assume the company goes out of business today and then calculate how much it owes as of this date. Using actuarial tables, current pension plan provisions, the current employee and retiree personnel database, and other data — and a multitude of assumptions — a company can make a guess at what it will have to pay current and future retirees year by year over the next 20 or 30 years.

Once this estimate of year-by-year future payments is completed, the next step is to estimate what the accumulated promises are worth today. In other words, how much money would the company have to set aside today in a lump sum amount in order to meet all these future retirement payments? A mathematical technique called discounted present value is used to make this determination. The future amounts are discounted to a present value using an assumed investment rate. The assumed investment rate is a very important number because small changes in it can have a large impact on what the company says it owes its plan participants.

What has just been outlined is a reasonable approach to a complex problem, but another factor should be remembered. Assumptions are used in the calculations and, as such, can either be conservative or aggressive. So the attitude of senior executives and that of the plan's actuary will also influence the size of the estimate. In some cases, executive attitude can change the size of the estimate significantly.

Consider the selection of the investment rate used in the discounting process. To illustrate the point, think about the college education fund described earlier in this chapter. Instead of the parents setting it up, however, say the grandparents wanted to set aside a single, lump-sum amount today that would be invested and would grow to a sufficient size to pay the college tuition for their grandchild he or she became 18. Furthermore, say the grandparents wanted this amount to grow to $28,000. Now, $28,000 probably won't be enough to pay for four years of college in eighteen years, but for this example it will do.

The amount that should be set aside today to meet this future commitment depends on the investment rate used. The higher the assumed investment rate, the lower the amount that must be set aside. The exact figures for $28,000 in 18 years are:

Assumed annual investment rate	Amount to set aside today
3%	$16,447
8%	7,005
20%	1,052

If the grandparents assumed the lump sum would earn 20 percent a year for the next 18 years, they would need to set aside only $1,052 in the education fund. That amount, earning at a rate of 20 percent a year, will grow to $28,000 in 18 years. On the other hand, if the grandparents assumed the money to be set aside would earn only 3 percent a year, then they must come up with $16,447. What's causing the lump sum amount to go down as the investment rate goes up? Simply the compounding factor. The higher the investment rate, the faster the earnings on the earnings compound. So, how much has to be set aside — $1,052 or $16,447? It all depends on what the grandparents use for an investment rate.

Senior executives also select an investment rate (within government mandated guidelines) when they calculate pension plan liabilities. If they are aggressive — that is, they select a higher investment rate — they can say that less money needs to be set aside today in order to live up to the company's future pension promises. When this lesser amount is compared to the assets in the pension fund, the pension plan will look better funded than if a lower, more conservative investment rate was used. If the plan looks better funded, then the company can reduce or eliminate its contributions to the pension fund.

Does this sound too complex? Well, just think of the lump-sum amount the company says it owes its plan participants as a mark on the wall of our water tank. It is sort of a depth gauge, which to a large extent can be moved up or down by senior executives based on the assumptions they make. Normally the mark on the wall is called the "present value of accumulated plan benefits." This number for a pension fund appears in the company's annual report, generally located in the section entitled "notes to consolidated financial statements" under the sub heading of "employee benefit plans."

The bottom line is simply this: A company can control the size of the contributions it makes into the pension fund by fiddling with the assumptions it uses to determine how much it owes plan participants. By adjusting the mark on the wall downward and by comparing this new mark with the level of money in the tank (the assets in the pension fund), senior executives can say they don't have to turn on the pump (increase contributions) because the level is where it is supposed to be.

Pension fund administration is quite straightforward when it is thought of as inflows, outflows, a mark on the wall, and some money already in the tank. To reinforce the concepts, consider a scenario in which a company goes bankrupt. If the company has been making the proper contributions to the fund all along, if the pension fund's assets are properly managed, and if all the assumptions those in charge of the pension fund have made prove correct, there is nothing to worry about. Think it through. First, the flow of money into the tank from the company's contributions probably will stop, as the company would be hard pressed to make any more contributions. However, the outflow (benefit payments) continues and, in fact, may increase as people faced with layoffs opt for early retirement. Although the inflow from investments made with pension assets continues to help replenish the tank, the outflow is larger, and gradually the tank is drained of money.

The pension promise will be safe, however, if the amount of money in the tank when the company went bankrupt plus all the future earnings on pension assets is enough to make all the retirement payments for as long as the plan participants live. Indeed, if everything was done just right, the last pensioner will die at the exact time the last drop of cash is drained from the tank.

The condition just described refers to a pension fund that is "fully funded." That is, the market value of assets in the pension fund equals the mark on the wall, which is a measure of the plan's liabilities if the company went out of business today.

If the company was not making the appropriate contributions before it went bankrupt, or if the pension fund sustained significant investment losses after the company went bankrupt, the level of assets in the pension fund would be below the mark on the wall. The plan's liabilities (what it promised plan participants) would exceed the pension fund's assets. There is not enough money in the tank to make good on all the retirement promises. The plan is underfunded. Net result: the tank will run dry before all the promises are kept.

Of course, this underfunded pension plan may get lucky and later earn more on its investments than originally forecasted, or retirees may die faster than expected, but which plan participant wants to count on these things occurring in the hope that their retirement income is secure? If a company does go bankrupt and has an underfunded pension fund, and if the plan is covered, it might fall into the so-called Pension Benefit Guaranty Corporation (PBGC) "safety net." The downside is benefits might be cut. (More about this in Chapter 3.)

EXCESS ASSETS

A more pleasant situation occurs when the assets in the pension fund are greater that the pension plan's liabilities. In the context of our water tower analogy, this is where the amount of money in the tank is above the mark on the wall. In this scenario the pension plan is well-funded. The pension fund has so-called "excess" assets.

Excess assets can come from three sources: conservative funding policies that caused a company to increase the amount of money it contributed to the pension fund; limited benefit provisions that resulted in smaller outflows to retirees; and/or excellent investment returns on the assets in the pension fund that increased the inflow from this source.

Excess assets are a good thing. First, they allow a company to take what is called in the industry a contribution holiday. Including expected investment earnings, there is more than enough money in the pension fund to keep all the pension promises the company has made to plan participants. That being the case, there is no need for the company to make further contributions; hence, they can stop. Second, excess assets provide a cushion against fluctuating investment returns — and investment returns do fluctuate, sometimes greatly. The cushion of excess assets provides added security that the pension promise will be kept over the long run even if short-term investment returns are negative. Third, excess assets in the pension fund provide the company with the opportunity to increase retirement income benefits without adversely affecting corporate earnings. For example, inflation, while trending downward these past five or so years, has not been zero. Indeed, the cost of living as measured by the Consumer Price Index has increased by about 20 percent. For people living on a fixed income, that's a hard hit. With excess assets in its pension fund a company might be willing to give retirees an increase to make up for this loss of purchasing power. Finally, excess assets provide the company with the opportunity to offer enhanced early retirement benefits in order to ease the financial pain of corporate restructuring.

With excess assets in a pension fund, everyone wins — the company doesn't have to make any more contributions and the employees and retirees can receive increased benefits. But even if the company chooses not to increase benefits, plan participants can rest a little easier with the knowledge they have a cushion in their pension fund.

With that cushion they have a greater degree of assurance that their benefits will in fact be paid. In today's volatile investment environment, that is worth a lot.

SELF-SERVING MANAGEMENT

It is an unfortunate fact of life: Wherever there is money and power, there will be someone who wants to take advantage of their position for personal gain. A self-serving chief investment officer given the responsibility for investing your pension fund's assets spells trouble. Taken to the extreme, pension funds can become mere stepping stones for these self-serving executives to advance their own personal wealth and careers. The pension fund becomes the chief investment officer's personal wealth foundation.

This is truly a very sad state of affairs. In this scenario, pension fund expenses are likely to go up — and go up a lot. Passing out lucrative contracts and generally acting like "Santa Claus" with pension expense money is one of the ways a chief investment officer can accumulate IOUs. It's called back-scratching. The chief investment officer gives a lucrative pension fund account to a supplier and expects that supplier to do something for him or her in return. Since pension fund contracts can be worth millions of dollars, there is ample incentive for suppliers to play the game. So the first thing that is likely to happen is that less money will flow into the pension fund because it is being diverted into lucrative contracts given to pension fund suppliers.

The second thing that is likely to happen is that investment decisions will be tainted by the chief investment officer's personal goals. Rather than evaluating the merits of an investment from the plan participant's viewpoint, all that will matter is what's in it for the chief investment officer. True, a chief investment officer could be very concerned about the pension fund and still give himself or herself a personal edge in awarding contracts. It does not have to be an either/or choice. Over time, however, and especially when faced with a particularly attractive personal arrangement, the pension fund is bound to lose and in go the shaky investments.

Furthermore, the self-serving investments probably will not perform very well. Remember, these investments were not selected based on their expected return relative to the risk taken, but rather on what the investment could do to advance the career or wealth of those in charge of the pension fund. In time, huge losses could suddenly appear and the size of the pension fund start to shrink — and it could shrink radically as the poor investment decision "time bombs" go off. The pension fund becomes smaller and smaller as this self-serving cancer eats away at the fund's financial health.

Who Loses?

Common sense says if wrongdoers siphon money out of the pension fund there will be less money in the fund than there would have been were it not for the wrongdoing. Less money in the pension fund means:

+ The pension promise is less secure.
+ Cost of living increases might have to be delayed or eliminated.
+ General improvements in pension benefits might have to be delayed or eliminated.
+ Early retirement programs that are designed to lessen the impact on employees from downsizing might have to be cut back or eliminated.
+ Benefits might be cut if a grossly underfunded plan is terminated and it slips into the PBGC safety net.

Sure, the company may make up the shortfall by increasing its contributions. It also might give retirees inflation adjustments in their pension checks or offer enhanced early retirement plans. But where is the money going to come from? Reduced corporate earnings? Maybe, but that will impact senior executive compensation packages and might upset shareowners. From a reduction in other corporate expenses? Again, perhaps, but cutbacks in other areas of the company might hamper long-term corporate growth prospects.

Faced with a pension fund shortfall, senior executives are more likely to change the pension fund's assumptions to hide it; increase the risk level in the pension fund investments in hopes that riskier investments will earn a higher return to make up the shortfall; or just do nothing. Some senior executives might reason that, if all else fails, the PBGC will step in, so why should they worry?

Who loses when self-serving employees take over a pension fund? You do, although you probably won't realize it right away. Five years down the road the cracks will start appearing. In another five years, perhaps just when you are getting ready to retire, the fund falls apart. This is why you must take an interest in what goes on in your pension fund *right now*. It is in your own self-interest to do so.

CHAPTER 3

The Present Role of the Government

The system of checks and balances the government has set up to help protect the pension promise may not be as solid as you had hoped.

This chapter will point out some of the cracks. Remember, however, that the issues discussed here are in transition. By the time you read this chapter the situation may have gotten worse — or better, although the latter prospect could be wishful thinking.

EMPLOYEE RETIREMENT INCOME SECURITY ACT (ERISA)

ERISA was enacted by Congress in 1974 and amended several times since then. This landmark piece of legislation sets out some rules for the administration of those pension plans and pension funds covered by it. ERISA also established two governmental agencies and requires the disclosure of certain pension fund information.

With respect to whom the assets of your pension fund are to be invested for, ERISA is quite clear. Pension plan assets are to be invested *solely* for the benefit of the plan's participants. Not for the benefit of the company; not for the benefit of senior executives; and not to advance the careers or personal wealth of company employees — solely for plan participants, and with the care, skill, and prudence of someone who is familiar with such matters. The exact words are:

... a fiduciary shall discharge his duties with respect to a plan solely in the interest of the participants and beneficiaries and —

1. for the exclusive purpose of:
     (*i*) providing benefits to participants and their beneficiaries; and
     (*ii*) defraying reasonable expenses of administering the plan;
2. with the care, skill, prudence, and diligence under the circumstances then prevailing that a prudent man acting in a like capacity and familiar with such matters would use in the conduct of an enterprise of a like character and with like aims; ...

ERISA is also quite clear about the protection extended to those individuals who report wrongdoing:

It shall be unlawful for any person to discharge, fine, suspend, expel, or discriminate against any person because he has given information or has testified or is about to testify in any inquiry or proceeding relating to the chapter or the Welfare and Pension Plans Disclosure Act.

These are grand words. The truth, however, is that powerful or clever people can skirt both these sections with relative impunity. First, according to a legal expert, ERISA's antiretaliation protection does not extend to an employee who reports wrongdoing to internal company investigators. Protection under ERISA seems to be so narrowly written that the employee must go to the Department of Labor, which administers ERISA, with his or her allegations. If an individual is foolish or naive enough to tell senior executives about the questionable activities, he or she is exposed to possible corporate retaliation without the protection of ERISA.

Even if an employee went to the Department of Labor, though, senior executives could still retaliate in many subtle ways. For example, they could transfer the whistle-blower to a distant outpost because of the "demands of the business" or give the individual gradually poorer and poorer appraisals until the person gets the ax at some respectable period of time in the future. Then it's up to the now ex-employee to prove the two are connected. Good luck. With this type of retaliation waiting for a pension fund employee, the temptation is to just look the other way or move on to a more ethical environment — which in turn allows senior executives to ignore the first section of ERISA's grand words about how pension assets are to be invested.

Moreover, some companies explicitly protect their senior executives and board members from the implications of breaches of ERISA. Consider this statement:

> *The Corporation shall indemnify* any person who was or is a party or is threatened to be made a party to any threatened, pending, or completed action, suit or proceeding, whether civil, criminal, administrative or investigative, . . . arising under the Employee Retirement Income Security Act of 1974 . . . against expenses (including attorney's fees), judgments, fines, penalties, taxes and amounts paid in settlement . . . by reason of the fact that he is or was a fiduciary, disqualified person or party in interest with respect to an employee benefit plan covering employees of the corporation . . . [Emphasis added.]

Particularly egregious violations might cause this company to rethink its protection and the company may indeed initiate legal action against an offending party, but it is doubtful that a company will turn on its most senior executives. What chief executive officer wants to see his or her company involved in a scandal? Who knows — maybe others were negligent in their supervision, or worse, had their own hands in the pension fund cookie jar. If a company's management so decides, no one on the outside is likely to be any the wiser about what really went on.

Sure, if the wrongdoers are discovered they might be asked to move on. But so what? If the scams work, finding another source of income will not be high on their list of worries. Their concerns about income may well have become academic by then.

PENSION AND WELFARE BENEFITS ADMINISTRATION (PWBA)

This agency was established when ERISA was passed in 1974. It is part of the U.S. Department of Labor.

The PWBA has two stated goals: (1) protecting the rights and financial security of employee benefit plan participants and beneficiaries; and (2) assuring the integrity and effective management of the private pension and welfare benefit plan system.

The agency is engaged in several activities, including: formulating current and future policy; conducting research; issuing regulation and technical guidance concerning ERISA requirements; enforcing

ERISA requirements; and assisting and educating the employee benefit community about ERISA

The PWBA also conducts civil and criminal investigations into
pension plan operations and investments. So there is at least one
government organization that has the responsibility to watch over a
pension fund's assets. Indeed, this is the agency a whistle-blowing employee would contact with allegations of wrongdoing.

But consider this:

> Most pension money is well-managed. Still, almost every week, the de-
> partment discloses that yet another employer has been stealing from a
> plan. By stealing I mean illegally borrowing assets, paying excessive
> fees to plan administrators — as well as an astonishing amount of out-
> right theft. What the inspector general pointed out so dramatically was
> that the Labor Department has only about 300 investigators. They can
> review fewer than 1% of the plans each year.[1]

With such limited resources in the face of such a large task, and
with additional budget cuts always a possibility, there is only so much
the PWBA investigators can do. To help improve effectiveness, an investigator in the PWBA asked the author to help develop a list of
clues or flash points that would serve as signals that something within
a pension fund was not right. Seeing these clues or flash points, the
PWBA could then conduct a more detailed review.

The author gave the request a great deal of thought, but finally
decided the exercise was meaningless. Clever and determined employees could effectively hide most of the wrongdoing from the view
of even the most diligent outside investigator. He or she can simply
recast the questionable activities as judgment calls and hide the connections which would point to wrongdoing, and then destroy any in-
criminating documents. If that desire to cover-up spreads to senior
executives who want to avoid embarrassment, it then becomes virtually impossible for anyone from the outside to detect wrongdoing in
a pension fund.

Hiring more PWBA investigators is not the answer. The best
and cheapest protection is to make fundamental changes within the
pension fund itself.

---

1. "How to Be Sure Your Pension Will Be There When You Retire" (an interview with
    Karen W. Ferguson, director of the Pension Rights Center), *Money*, December 1990.

PENSION BENEFIT GUARANTY
CORPORATION (PBGC)

The PBGC is another U.S. government agency set up by ERISA. It was designed to help protect those individuals who participate in private defined benefit pension plans. This is how the PBGC describes itself:

> [The] PBGC is a federal agency that insures and protects pension benefits in certain pension plans. If your plan is insured by PBGC, we guarantee your pension benefits, up to certain legal limits. If your employer has financial difficulty and cannot fund the plan, and the plan does not have enough money to pay all promised benefits, your plan ends (plan termination). PBGC then takes the plan over as trustee and begins to pay pension benefits.[2]

The protection provided by the PBGC acts as sort of a safety net. If a company is unable to live up to its pension promise and the plan is taken over, the PBGC will pay a certain level of benefits to plan participants in those plans they cover. As of March 1995, the PBGC pays monthly benefits to about 174,000 retirees in 1,971 terminated plans. Another 200,000 participants in these terminated plans will be paid when they reach retirement age.

Most private defined benefit pension plans are covered by the PBGC. The exceptions are those plans sponsored by "professional service employers" with fewer than 26 employees, church groups, and governmental groups.

From the viewpoint of plan participants one of the most important areas of PBGC involvment is in pension plan terminations. Terminations can occur from actions taken either by the company or by the PBGC.

One reason the PBGC would terminate a pension plan is to protect its own interests. For example, a company whose pension fund is grossly underfunded (that is, the promises it has made its plan participants far exceed the money in the pension fund) may start to transfer corporate assets out of the company. If the PBGC sees this it may decide to initiate the termination of the pension plan and lay claim to the company's remaining assets before they all vanish. Taken to the extreme, if the PBGC waited there might be few remaining corporate

---

2. "Your Guaranteed Pension," Pension Benefit Guaranty Corporation, January 1995.

assets left to lay claim to. By making a preemptive strike, the PBGC
might secure more cash to help it make the basic pension payments it
promised.

> The Pension Benefit Guaranty Corp. filed a lawsuit to terminate the
> underfunded pension plan for New Valley Corp's Western Union op-
> erations, in the fourth-largest pension intervention ever undertaken
> by the federal agency . . . The plan for 16,000 Western Union em-
> ployees and retirees is underfunded by $389 million. Currently, the
> pension agency expects to be liable for $178 million of that amount,
> but said that both the deficit and the agency's liability for it could
> grow in the future. "We must act now to prevent unreasonable loss to
> the federal insurance system, and ultimately, to taxpayers and pen-
> sioners," said Martin Slate, executive director of the agency.[3]

There could be several reasons why a company might want to
terminate its pension plan. The PBGC classifies these company-initi-
ated terminations as either standard terminations or distress terminations and treats each category somewhat differently.

In a standard termination the company must demonstrate to the
PBGC that there are enough assets in the pension fund to cover all
the benefits that were promised as of the date of termination. If the
plan qualifies, the company can proceed with the termination.

In a distress termination the employer wants to terminate its
pension plan but lacks the assets in the pension fund to cover all its
promises. In these cases, the employer now needs to demonstrate that
it is in such poor financial shape or the pension costs are so burdensome that unless it is allowed to jettison its pension obligations the
enterprise simply will not survive. The company would characterize
its request as a life-or-death situation for the business — terminate the
plan or the company goes bankrupt. Now comes the PBGC test: Are
there enough assets in the pension fund to at least cover the minimum
level of benefits guaranteed by the PBGC? (More about those levels
in a minute.) If there are enough assets to cover this bare minimum,
the PBGC lets the employer proceed as if it were a standard termination but obviously with a lower level of benefits. If there are not
enough assets to cover the PBGC guarantee, the PBGC steps in.
They make sure plan participants are at least paid that minimum

---

3. "U.S. Sues to Terminate Pension Plan of New Valley's Western Union Unit," *The Wall
    Street Journal*, October 18, 1994.

amount. The PBGC can then seek to recover the shortfall through various actions against the company. (There is more — much more — to the process, including the promises made by the company over and above the PBGC minimum, but at least this provides an overview of the relevant points. Readers who want more information should contact the PBGC, U.S. Department of Labor, Washington, D.C. 20210.)

If a defined benefit pension plan was terminated in 1995, the maximum monthly guarantee for a single life annuity with no survivor benefits would be:

Age	Maximum
65	$2573.86
62	2033.35
60	1673.01
55	1158.24

Source: "Facts," Pension Benefit Guaranty Corporation, March, 1995.

This raises an interesting question. If a governmental agency "guarantees" a certain level of benefits in a covered defined benefit pension plan, why should anyone be concerned about wrongdoing in a pension fund? After all, if the pension fund fails, the PBGC will step in.

Unfortunately, things are not as nice, tidy, and clean cut as that. Consider this. The PBGC may not have the financial resources in its "kitty" to make good on its promises. Remember, the PBGC already has taken over 1,971 plans with a commitment to 374,000 plan participants. The PBGC paid $721 million in benefits to retirees of terminated plans in fiscal 1994. The plans taken over were reported to have had pension fund assets totaling $8.7 billion. To cover the benefit level the PBGC guarantees, however, $9.2 billion is needed. That's a lot of plans, a lot of participants, and a deficit in the amount of assets (including accumulated premium payments, investment earnings, and securities) which the PBGC has to cover its commitments.

Some say the 50 most underfunded private pension plans should be included in the evaluation of the PBGC's financial soundness because they are potential PBGC customers. If these plans went under, the PBGC would have to pick up the pieces. How big is this overhang?

The Pension Benefit Guaranty Corp., the government agency that insures private pension plans, said underfunding at these 50 companies totaled $13.5 billion . . .[4]

And the shortfall for all pension plans insured by the PBGC, including the 50 most underfunded?

About 8 million people are covered by about 10,000 underfunded plans, which in 1994 had assets of $211 billion and benefit liabilities of $242 billion (for a deficit of $31 billion). They compromise one-fifth of all defined pension plans, PBGC said . . .[5]

Finally, just change a few assumptions used in these calculations to a worst-case scenario and soon you have another looming savings and loan size disaster. Presumably, if the PBGC went under the federal government would step in — so the ultimate liability lies with the taxpayers.

To be fair, others say, just lower benefits, pressure employers to fully fund their plans, increase the PBGC premiums, and as long as the economy keeps growing, the PBGC safety net will be secure. Perhaps. But the PBGC doesn't operate in a vacuum. Rules and changes have to be approved by Congress. Sure, the government could pass legislation requiring companies to become fully funded, but that risks pushing some companies into bankruptcy. The government could also stop a company's management from making more retirement promises than it has pension assets to keep, but even that proposal has been hotly resisted by interest groups. And raising insurance premiums to help cover the shortfall? Healthy pension funds question, with some degree of justification, why they should have to foot the bill to bail out defunct pension plans whose management might have been just taking advantage of the PBGC system to begin with. There you have the parameters of the debate.

This is a dynamic situation, and by the time this book is published the PBGC's financial situation will have changed either for the better or worse. This discussion, however, sets the scope of the problem.

Another issue vital to anyone who puts their trust in the government to protect his or her retirement well-being is the size of the

---

4. "Underfunding in Pension Plans Narrowed in 1994," *The Wall Street Journal*, December 7, 1995.
5. "Pension Fund Shortfall Declined in 1994, First Drop in a Decade," *Investor's Business Daily*, November 30, 1995.

guarantee provided by the PBGC. Here's what some people had to say about their experiences.

> Mr. Christie, who lives in North Merrick, N.Y., had been promised that if he left Pan Am, he would get a pension of more than $1,000 a month when he turned 55 in late 1991. But the federal Pension Benefit Guaranty Corp., which took over the Pan Am plan, determined that it is obligated to pay him only $596 a month. After being out of work for 10 months, Mr. Christie has taken a job as an aircraft-maintenance analyst at less than half his former pay.[6]

Here is another personal experience.

> Frank Dysart, a former $60,000-a-year Eastern pilot on disability retirement since 1989 because of an inoperable ruptured disk in his back and a heart condition, says he was assured by the PBGC and Eastern's management that his disability pay wouldn't be affected. But the PBGC slashed it to $984 a month from $2,200.[7]

Thousands of people can be affected by the reduction in promised benefits when the PBGC takes over a plan:

> . . . about 2,000 pilots and approximately 300 flight engineers will receive reduced benefits because of caps on the monthly amounts that the [PBGC] guarantees.[8]

And the surprises extend to those who took early retirement:

> For people who took early retirement in their 50's, as more and more have been doing (in 1992 more than a third of American men ages 55 through 64 were not working), the guarantee may be as low as $12,000 a year. The fact that your employer promised you a bigger pension to persuade you to take early retirement will not help you if the company goes bust with an underfunded plan.[9]

The safety net provided by the PBGC is fine. But the best protection a plan participant can have that the pension promise will be kept is a well-funded pension fund that is properly managed and free from wrongdoing by self-serving company employees.

---

6. "Imperiled Promises — Risk to Retirees Rise as Firms Fail to Fund Pensions They Offer," *The Wall Street Journal*, February 4, 1993.
7. Ibid.
8. "Pan Am to Pay Pension Benefits via U.S. Agency," *The Wall Street Journal*, October 4, 1994.
9. Martin Mayer, "Pensions: The Naked Truth," *Modern Maturity*, February/March 1993.

SECTION 415 LIMITATIONS AND
SUPPLEMENTAL PLANS

Most employees who are thinking about retirement will know exactly what monetary benefits they can expect when they retire, right down to the penny. It may come as a surprise to some, however, that not all of that money will come from the pension fund. If a company promises a retirement income higher than what the government deems "reasonable," the excess is generally paid from the company's checkbook under a supplemental plan especially set up by the company for this contingency.

This method of retirement payment is a result of the government's attempt to block senior executives from receiving what the government considers overly generous retirement income at the taxpayer's expense. The restrictions are spelled out in Section 415 of the tax code and hence are known as "Section 415 limitations." The IRS gets involved because of the tax-exempt status of the pension fund and the contributions made to it.

To simplify discussion of these limitations, the industry has come up with some terms. Since a pension fund qualifies for favorable tax treatment (within certain limits, company contributions are tax deductible and earnings within the pension fund are not taxed), that portion of a retiree's pension which is paid from the pension fund is deemed to have come from a qualified plan. The additional payment that makes up the balance of what was promised a plan participant comes from what is called the nonqualified plan. A retiree's check stubs will probably even reflect these differences.

Age at retirement, salary, a host of other factors (including such esoteric information as past employee stock ownership plan distributions), and, the most important determinant, IRS maximum salary restrictions, enter into the calculations to determine the maximum amount that can be paid from the pension fund.

In the past only the most top-level executives were affected by Section 415 limitations. But with the government lowering the maximum amount of salary that can enter into the Section 415 calculations (they want more tax revenues, and this is a back door approach to get them), and with all the early retirement programs going on, many lower to middle level management employees (now retirees) could be affected as well.

The problem is simply this: The supplemental portion of the retirement promise is even more at risk than the amount paid from the
pension fund. There is no pension fund to help secure this portion of
the company's retirement promise, nor is there even a PBGC safety
net. The payments are made from the company's checkbook, and no-
body knows if the company will even be around over the next 10 or
20 years, the time frame over which a retiree might expect to receive
the payments.

The most senior executives often recognize the risk and take
care of themselves. They are not dumb. They apparently don't trust
those who will follow them so, while they are in power, some of
them get their companies to set up special funds or trust accounts that
will help to secure their supplemental payments when they retire.
One such plan is called a "rabbi" trust (so named because of the first
beneficiary of such a trust). For these most senior executives, money
is set aside today in the "rabbi" trust to fund their supplemental
benefits, which will be paid in the future. Such a trust may not exist
for middle to lower level employees. The author tried to get information about the other trusts, plans, or agreements which secured
the supplemental payments for other retirees at his company. As a
plan participant who receives a supplemental payment, he thought
he was entitled to this information. The company's reply? "Please
note that federal pension law does not require us to provide you with
information concerning plans or programs in which you are not a
participant."

Returning to the discussion of Section 415 limitations, the author believes the government's actions are misguided and have unin-
tended consequences. The constant tightening of the Section 415
limitations causes two things to happen. First, more and more retirees
are pushed into nonqualified plans, which have little or no protection
or security. The most senior executives, the alleged targets of the limitations, however, can find ways to protect their own interests. They
can set up supplemental plans for themselves, which they do not have
to disclose to participants in other supplemental plans offered by the
company. Second, the government is undermining the security of the
pension fund by reducing the amount of personal stake a senior executive has in the fund's financial well-being. Right now, much of a senior executive's retirement well-being comes from wealth he or she
can accumulate along the way in terms of salary and performance

bonuses, and from the supplemental plans the company sets up for them, not from the pension fund. Put yourself in the position of these senior executives. If you were faced with a choice of enhancing the security of the pension fund (in which you have little personal stake because of Section 415 limitations) or with increasing corporate earnings (and thus your own performance bonus or even saving your own job), which would you choose?

INTERNAL REVENUE SERVICE (IRS)

Yes, this feared agency also plays a role in the pension fund. Since the contributions a company makes to a pension fund are tax deductible, the IRS keeps a watchful eye to make sure the government isn't getting shortchanged by a company contributing too much money into its pension fund.

The IRS has several ways to influence the size of a company's contributions. One way is to challenge the assumptions a company uses to determine the size of its contributions. If a company lowers the rate of return its pension fund is expected to earn on its investments, the size of the contributions the company must make to its pension fund will increase, all else being equal. So if the IRS wants to minimize the size of a company's contributions they will argue for a higher assumed rate of return on investments. Indeed, the IRS has even gone to court to try to force companies to use more aggressive (they would say more realistic) assumptions.

But companies are put in a box:

> Corporations complain that they are victims of conflicting signals from government regulatory agencies. The Internal Revenue Service tries to limit corporate tax deductions for pension-fund contributions by challenging companies that it thinks are using assumptions that are too low. The PBGC, in contrast, pushes them to put more money into their pension funds, hoping to limit the number of underfunded plans it has to bail out.[10]

The perverse nature of the IRS's actions are taken to the extreme when some companies try to add money to a badly underfunded pension fund:

---

10. "Retirees at Risk — Hopeful Assumptions Let Firms Minimize Pension Contributions," *The Wall Street Journal*, September 2, 1993.

A number of employers with underfunded plans have complained to us that if they fully fund those plans, they cannot deduct contributions to their companion defined contribution plans because of the 25% limit on contributions applicable to employers with defined contribution and defined benefit plans.[11]

The interest of the IRS in limiting tax deductibility is expected and proper. It is also natural for the PBGC to want companies to make sufficient contributions into the pension fund to ensure that the promised benefits are in fact paid so that the PBGC won't have to step in. Each agency is playing its mandated role. In the author's opinion, however, the IRS appears to sometimes work at cross-purposes with the interests of plan participants who would like to see increased contributions into a pension fund and a well-funded pension plan.

A PLAN PARTICIPANT'S ACCESS TO INFORMATION

The company is required to provide the IRS and the Department of Labor with certain information about its pension fund. The vehicle for transmitting this information is called Form 5500 Report. Plan participants have the right to see this information — it's the law. A plan participant should ask the company's benefits department for a copy.

The problem is that for most plan participants this information is confusing and not very useful. The format resembles a tax form and is full of hard to understand encryptions. The important information, such as pension fund and investment manager performance results, is missing. It is virtually impossible to determine whether the senior executives in charge of the pension fund's investments are doing a good job or not.

A plan participant can ask his or her company for additional information, but they are not legally bound to provide it. For example, in late 1993 the author became concerned about reports in the investment press that the pension fund in which he is a participant had written down its real estate investments by hundreds of millions of dollars. He was also concerned about an informal report that the

---

11. Quote attributed to Martin Slate, current director of the PBGC, "Congress May Kill Contribution Tax," *Pension & Investments*, June 14, 1993.

pension fund significantly underperformed its own bogie, a bench-mark composed of other, similar pension funds the company's deci-sion makers believed they could beat. A quick review of the company's annual report also showed the fund was shrinking when the stock and bond markets were moving higher. He was concerned and wrote ask-ing for additional information and asked that certain questions about the administration of the fund also be answered. Here is the reply he received from the company's Secretary of the Benefits Committee:

> The information you are seeking is *beyond the scope of ERISA's disclosure requirements.* As a result, I regret that we are unable to respond to your requests. [Emphasis added.]

At the minimum, the minutes of pension fund committee meet-ings should have contained the information he was looking for. Here's the reply he got when he asked for access:

> *Under company policy,* we are not able to provide you the opportunity to review the material you requested . . . [Emphasis added]

So he wrote to the U.S. Department of Labor and asked for their help. Their reply was:

> The Employee Retirement Income Security Act of 1974 provides that a plan administrator, upon written request of any participant or bene-ficiary must furnish copies of certain plan documents. However, an individual participant is not, as a matter of law, entitled to internal doc-uments pertaining to the investment activities of the pension plan. Dis-closure of this type of information is not required by ERISA, and is *purely voluntary* on the part of the pension plan. [Emphasis added.]

This is wrong. Plan participants should be entitled to know what is going on within their pension funds, and that information should be provided in an easily understood format.

CHAPTER 4

Investment Decisions

This chapter goes step by step through some of the major investment decisions facing the people who manage a pension fund's assets. It is important to spotlight these decisions because it is in the cracks and crannies of detail where the wrongdoers hide.

DIVERSIFICATION

Pension funds often invest in a variety of instruments — common stocks, bonds, real estate, international investments, venture capital, and temporary investments, such as T-bills and CDs. The decision makers could put all of the pension fund's money into one type of investment and have the chance of making a killing, but if the assumptions used in the selection process were faulty, the pension fund could lose a lot of money and, as a result, seriously impair a plan participant's retirement security. Diversification is not a panacea, however; it doesn't eliminate the chance of a total disaster, just reduces its likelihood.

Figure 4–1 provides a picture of how diversification works. The top panel depicts the price pattern for one type of investment. As depicted, the market value of this investment fluctuates frequently — sometimes it is up, sometimes down. An individual who bought this investment when it was down and sold it when it was up could have made a lot of money. Someone who is perfect in calling the market has

FIGURE 4-1

How Diversification Works

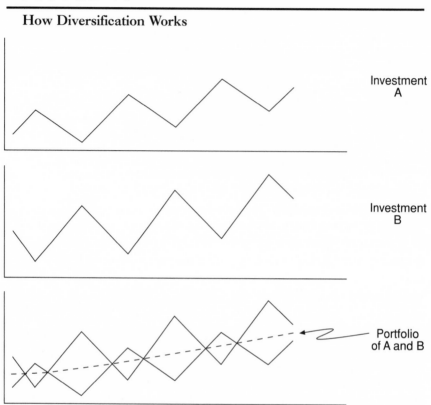

Investment
A

Investment
B

Portfolio
of A and B

no need to diversify — but who is that perfect? There are just too many unknowns. Moreover, not only does one have to be right in when to exit the market, one also must be correct in timing his or her re-entry. The author has seen some outstanding investors, but none were always 100 percent perfect.

Now look at the middle panel. This shows the change in market value from an entirely different type of investment. It too is very volatile, but when it is up, investment A tends to be down, and vice versa. In investment lingo they are negatively correlated investment types.

What if these two investments are combined into a portfolio? That is, if an investor puts 50 percent of his or her money into investment A and the remaining 50 percent into investment B, what happens to volatility? The bottom panel shows the answer. Combining 50 percent of investment A and 50 percent of investment B makes the resulting portfolio significantly less volatile than either A or B alone. The investor's portfolio has been diversified against the price actions of either A or B alone.

A reduction in volatility occurs only if the investments tend to perform differently from one another — that is, if one is up while the other is down, and vice versa. If they move together in lockstep, combining the two into a portfolio will not reduce volatility, just average it.

Diversification does work. It helped the author's pension fund (and others', too), for example, during the stock market crash of October 1987. Sure, the value of the pension fund's stock investments declined sharply, but mitigating against that decline were increases in bond prices and foreign currencies — both of which were well represented in the fund. Despite one of the worst stock market crashes in history, the company's pension fund was up about 5 percent for the year.

ASSET MIX

Most decision makers who are responsible for overseeing pension fund investments would agree that diversification in a pension fund is a desirable thing. But which investment types should be included and how much of the pension fund's assets should be allocated to each?

First, consider which types of investments should be included in a pension fund. There are a multitude of different choices. Some pension fund decision makers decide which investment types should be included by following the trend. Whatever seems to be hot at the moment gets included in the fund. Psychologically, it's easy to sell someone on an investment idea that has already shown a great deal of profit; there is some positive history to base a decision on. Smart management, however, would include a new investment type if, and only if, it would benefit the pension fund by (1) improving return expectations; (2) reducing risk exposure; or (3) providing a combination of both. For example, there would be no reason to add an investment type to the pension fund if its addition was expected to lower the fund's return and increase its risk.

The next decision is how much of the pension fund's money should be allocated to each of the selected investment types. This decision depends upon many factors, including:

- Expected performance of each investment type.
- Extent to which each investment type complements, balances, or is contrary to the other types.
- Funded status of the pension plan.
- Size and timing of future benefit payments.
- Financial health of the company.
- Risk tolerance of those making the decision.

These two issues — which investment types to include and how much of the pension fund's money to allocate to each — were presented as separate decisions. In reality, the pension fund decision makers will reach a conclusion on both at the same time after they have conducted an asset allocation study. An asset allocation study uses various assumptions and produces a number of alternative mixes of different investment types. The process has often been described as being similar to baking a cake. By varying the ingredients the baker can blend different flavors and textures, several of which might appeal to the decision maker's taste.

The mechanics are rather straightforward. However, it is the assumptions that control the results. Simply changing the expected return and risk characteristics for a specific investment type can bias the entire asset allocation study. Senior executives who are supposed to oversee the pension fund's investment process might not realize this and spend a great deal of time learning about the study procedures. They completely ignore what analyses (if any) went into the development of the assumptions. The person who is conducting the study is supposed to be scrupulously honest in making these assumptions. In reality, personal bias can enter into the study. The assumptions, and hence the results, can be manipulated by a self-serving chief investment officer for personal gain.

The decision makers would then evaluate the risk/return trade-offs offered by each of the alternative mixes and settle on the one mix they think best achieves the objectives outlined in the asset allocation study. This mix is called the pension fund's normal asset mix. It specifies how much of the pension fund's assets should be invested in each investment type in order to achieve the objectives outlined in the asset allocation study consistent with the assumptions that were made and over the time frame specified in the study. Every well-managed pension fund should conduct an asset allocation study. If they don't, they'll be managing the pension assets by the seat of their pants. That could be dangerous for plan participants.

A pension fund's normal asset mix might look like this:

Investment Type	Percent of Pension Fund Assets to be Invested in each
Stocks	
Domestic	47%
International	15
Bonds	
Domestic	30
International	0
Real estate	5
Venture capital	3
Cash	0
	100%

Stocks, bonds, and real estate are familiar investment alternatives; venture capital may not be. Venture capitalists are financial intermediaries who raise money from pension funds, insurance companies, banks, and wealthy individuals and invest it in new startup companies or smaller, rapidly growing companies. If these ventures grow and prosper, their value increases. At some point the venture capitalist would take the small company public (sell shares in an initial public offering, which will be described in a later chapter) and realize a profit. After taking a cut, the venture capitalist would pass along the remaining profit to the institutions and individuals who put up the capital. Venture capital investments are as straightforward as that.

The pension fund's normal asset mix is a guideline. It remains unchanged until a new asset allocation study is conducted. Of course, once investments are made the ever-changing market value of those investments, as well as the decisions by management, can cause the actual asset mix to differ from the normal asset mix. But a difference between the normal asset mix and the actual asset mix is not necessarily bad. (More on this in a minute.)

How important is the asset mix decision? Extremely important! For large pension funds the asset mix decision is often the single most important investment decision. Studies have shown that over 80 percent of a pension fund's total return can be explained by this one decision. Stop and think about that — over 80 percent of a pension fund's total return can be attributed to deciding which investment types to invest in and how much of the pension fund's assets to invest in each.

ASSET MIX RANGES

Most pension funds will establish ranges around these normal positions within which they will allow the actual mix to vary. These ranges play an important role in allowing the decision makers flexibility to take advantage of dynamic investment market conditions while at the same time not letting the pension fund's overall strategy be blown too far off course.

As an analogy, consider the annual Mackinaw Island sailboat race, which traverses almost the entire length of Lake Michigan — from Chicago to Mackinaw, Michigan. The objective is clear: Reach Mackinaw as quickly as you can. However, the racers also know that wind conditions will vary and the weather might change suddenly. Lake Michigan can be particularly treacherous. A straight-line course might be plotted, but the racers have to remain flexible to take advantage of the currents and prevailing winds, and be ready to deal with the unexpected.

The same is true with a pension fund. The decision makers should know where they want to go. If all the assumptions made in the asset allocation study prove correct, following the normal asset mix will get them there. However, investment waters are no less uncertain or less treacherous than the waters of Lake Michigan. The ranges around the normal asset mix allow the pension fund decision makers the flexibility to take advantage of the prevailing environment without straying too far from their guideline — the normal asset mix.

The width of the ranges are normally set based upon senior management's assessment of the chief investment officer's investment skills in timing investments, the volatility of the investment categories, and the company's ability to kick in more money should the chief investment officer not be the genius he or she is perceived to be.

INVESTMENT STRATEGIES

Once the decision makers have decided that a certain percentage of the pension fund's assets should be invested in a particular investment type, say common stocks, a whole host of other questions arise. In what areas of the stock market should that money be invested? How? With whom? When? The answer to all those questions is outlined in an investment strategy. Each investment type in a pension fund — stocks, bonds, real estate, venture capital, and temporary investments — should have a written strategy for allocating the money to be invested. After the asset mix, the investment strategy has the next largest impact on a pension fund's total return.

On the surface, developing an investment strategy for each investment type may seem like a daunting task. A large pension fund may have billions of dollars allocated to a single category, and the number of alternative ways to invest that money are mind-boggling. Appendix 1 at the end of this chapter provides some examples of the alternatives.

Here are the most important factors to consider when developing an investment strategy:

+ Efficiency of the investment category.
+ Ability of the pension fund decision makers to identify skillful managers.
+ Proportion of the pension fund's assets allocated to a particular investment category.
+ Level of risk the pension fund decision makers are willing to take.
+ Ways in which the investment manager's methods and styles complement, balance, or are contrary to each other.

A few of these factors need to be explained. "Efficiency of the investment category" is a shorthand way of referring to how fast information is reflected in the prices of the assets in that category. If it takes a long time for information to be reflected in prices, that category is often referred to as being inefficient. There is an opportunity for someone with superior knowledge to get in early and make some money before other investors get and react to the information. On the other hand, if prices adjust quickly to the new information (the category is efficient), the opportunity for making more money than what is offered by investing in the category itself may be limited.

Take common stocks as an example. If a drug company discovers a new anticancer drug, besides being a boon to mankind, that new drug will generate profits worth something to the stock's price. Suppose the company's stock is currently trading at $50 a share and a broker thinks this new drug will take the price to $75. He calls a friend first with this new information, and the friend buys some stock at $50 a share. The broker calls more and more people, and in turn they let their friends know. The information about this new cancer-fighting drug is now getting into the hands of investors, and they are acting on the information. The demand for the stock increases. Eventually, the stock's price reflects the information about the new drug and it trades at $75. (Crowd psychology will probably cause the price to overshoot before it eventually settles down to $75 per share.)

In an efficient market with many profit-motivated participants who have almost instantaneous access to all kinds of information, the price change might occur very quickly indeed. Not only will the demand for the shares increase dramatically as everyone receives the information almost simultaneously, but the supply of stock will dry up. For example, investors who held the stock would not sell it for $50 if they thought this new information would mean the stock is now "worth" $75.

The speed at which relevant information flows within a marketplace and the degree to which market participants take action varies between investment categories and even within sectors of a given category. A good investment strategist would be cognizant of these market quirks and would build a strategy that maximizes profit potential while minimizing risk. For example, in an efficient category where information is quickly reflected in market prices, an investment strategist might decide it is not worth the extra cost to pay someone to search for "bargains." In his or her opinion there aren't any — the current price already reflects all current information about the investment.

In that case, the investment strategy might be to invest the pension fund assets allocated to common stocks in a low-fee index fund that replicates the performance of the investment category, not even bothering to try to evaluate the individual investments within that category. Investment professionals call this passive investment management. Again, take common stocks as an example. A passive investment manager would construct a portfolio of stocks that would mimic the performance of a stock market index (say the Standard and Poor's 500). As the index goes up, so would the portfolio's value, in lockstep. And vice versa. On the other hand, active investment management requires an investment manager to decide which securities he or she thinks will outperform the rest. For common stock, an active investment manager would search through hundreds of stocks and invest in only those he or she felt would outperform the rest. It's a tough job, especially considering the number of very smart, well-financed investors with rapid access to information out there trying to do the same thing.

The second factor to explain is the "ways in which the investment manager's methods and styles complement, balance, or are contrary to each other." Common stocks again provide the example. An investor may decide that the stock market is not completely efficient — some investment managers have superior knowledge and do better than the market during some time frames. Therefore, it might be profitable to take the time and effort to seek out and hire investment managers who are able to build a portfolio of stocks that will provide the expectations for a higher than market return for the same amount of risk as a passive stock investment.

In our example, the hired investment manager's job is to decide which stocks to buy, when to buy them, and how much to buy. These are decisions every portfolio manager is faced with. To help in making those decisions, an investment manager normally adopts an investment philosophy which outlines how he or she thinks is the best way to make money in the stock market.

Some investment managers will say they only look for stocks whose companies are growing faster than the economy. They think that by concentrating their portfolios in these types of stocks the portfolio's performance over time will be better than the overall market. Others might say no, growth stocks (those described above) are way overpriced. The only way to really make money is to buy stocks that are cheap and/or to seek out investments in companies who have hidden assets that are not reflected in their stock price. These are generally called "value" managers. Still other investment managers will disagree with both approaches — growth stock and value stock investing. In fact, there is a seemingly endless variety of management styles.

Any long-term observer of the stock market will realize these investment styles seem to come into and go out of favor in cycles. At times, growth stock managers seem to outperform value managers, and vice versa.

How should an investment strategist factor these variables into the pension fund's investment strategy for common stocks? One way is to pick that style the strategist believes will provide the best return commensurate with the risk taken and then just stick with it through thick and thin. When the market is favoring the selected style, this is easy to do. The tough part is when the market turns against the style.

Another approach is to attempt to time the style; that is, to shift assets into the style which the strategist thinks will perform best over the future investment time horizon. Though sometimes tricky, this can be extremely profitable.

Yet another approach is to diversify away any unwanted risk associated with concentrating the fund's exposure to any one particular style. This is done by assembling a team of investment managers who are perceived to be the best in their styles, but whose styles differ from those of the other managers on the team. Then, when all the investments of all the selected managers are aggregated, the expected return of this aggregate is greater than investing in an index fund commensurate with the risk taken, net of all investment manager fees. To assemble such a team, a strategist must be cognizant of the "way in which the investment manager's methods and styles complement, balance, or are contrary to each other."

There are many, many investment strategies that can be developed. It really depends upon the creativity and experience of the strategist. The point is there is no one right way. However, flexibility and the willingness to change one's mind if the assumptions prove wrong are important to investment success. Appendix 2 to this chapter provides an example of an investment strategy the author developed several years ago for common stock investments.

All pension funds should have a written investment strategy for each of the investment categories in which the fund has invested pension assets. The investment strategy should hang together and make sense, and it should have stated performance benchmarks so that performance can be objectively measured. But plan participants do not have to become experts on investment strategies — all they really need to know is whether the strategy has worked or not. To determine that, those who manage a pension fund should be required to establish appropriate performance benchmarks for each investment alternative, and the results should be provided to plan participants.

MANAGER SELECTION

After an investment strategy has been developed for each of the investment alternatives, the next decision involves how to implement the strategy. Continuing with the common stock example, this could involve identifying and hiring investment managers who have experience investing in growth stocks, another set of managers who have experience in value stocks, and yet another manager who can construct and maintain an S&P 500 index fund.

The money allotted to growth stocks would then be divided among several growth stock managers, and it would be their responsibility to select which stocks to buy, when to buy them, and how much to buy. Guidelines, performance measurement, and review sessions are all part of the process.

On the other hand, the pension fund decision makers might want to manage at least some of the money in-house; that is, retain competent employees who will determine themselves which stocks to buy, when, and how much. The choice of whether to hire outside managers or to make the buy/sell/hold decisions on individual securities in-house often revolves on what style is to be employed, how much can be saved in investment management fees, and the expected performance results. And, of course, it doesn't have to be an all-or-nothing approach. Some activities can be managed in-house while others can be left to outside managers.

There are literally thousands of investment managers to choose from. In selecting an investment manager, these are the areas a decision maker in the pension fund would evaluate: (1) what type of investment style best fits the pension fund's investment strategy; (2) the investment manager's personnel (their skills and experience); (3) the investment process (the method the investment manager uses to select securities); and, (4) past performance. It may come as a surprise, but past performance is not always a reliable guide for predicting future performance. No one can say with 100 percent certainty that an investment manager's good historical performance will continue in the future. The investment manager may have been lucky, or the market environment may have favored the manager's investment style. Moreover, investment management firms change — sometimes ever so subtly. New staff members come on board, old hands leave, more clients come on-line, and the principals age and their outlooks and perceptions change. Some of this helps performance, some of it may hurt results. The point is that past performance may not be a very reliable guide for selecting an investment manager.

That leaves the investment manager's personnel and the investment management firm's investment process as deciding factors. But who is to say that one investment manager's personnel or investment process is better or worse than another's? Just because someone is an M.B.A. or a computer scientist or has the ability to market themselves doesn't necessarily mean they will be able to consistently make money for the pension fund.

The pension fund can and should go through the evaluation process, including on-site visits to interview all the investment professionals in the investment manager's organization. Nevertheless, investment manager selection should also be recognized for what it is — a subjective decision. Regardless of the spin a decision maker might try to put on it, in the final analysis, the decision to hire manager A instead of manager B is a judgment call, period.

If the selection process is subjective, the chief investment officer is in a position to decide which investment manager is selected. Most chief investment officers take their responsibilities seriously and try to do the best selection job they can. Others might be out for themselves. These people can manipulate the process to get a manager hired who in turn will "help" the chief investment officer in some personal way. The interest of plan participants and the pension fund come a distant second, if at all.

MANAGER GUIDELINES

A pension fund may hire 15 or 20 investment managers or more. Those managers generally work independently of each other and therefore are often unaware of the other's decisions. They need direction from the pension fund decision makers if the investment strategy is to achieve its objectives.

Guidelines, which indicate the role each investment manager is expected to play, are an integral part of the pension fund's efforts to coordinate the actions of the individual investment managers. In addition, guidelines provide a basis for the evaluation of investment manager performance.

Guidelines are intended to be dynamic, working documents. They are mutually agreed upon statements specifying the manager's responsibilities, investment style, and the expected risk and return characteristics of the account. They can be modified when required as agreed to by the investment manager and the pension fund decision makers. Guidelines need to be properly constructed, and there is a need to restate the fiduciary responsibilities of those involved in the process. They also should address ethical standards and provide the manager with a confidential source to talk to should the chief investment officer, or others in the company, start twisting arms to get "favors." The guidelines should be communicated to the investment managers from the highest levels of the corporation in order to underscore their importance to the company.

The reality of guidelines, however, is that many are designed by lawyers to be as general and innocuous as possible so as not to give rise to any "unnecessary" basis for lawsuits. Thus, in their preparation there is often a struggle between preparing specific, clear guidelines that are useful and those that are intended to protect particular interests.

INVESTMENT MANAGER PERFORMANCE REVIEW

Once an asset mix has been established, the investment strategies developed, the investment managers selected, and the manager guidelines established, the next thing on the list is to monitor the investment manager's performance results.

Performance evaluation is intended to help the pension fund decision makers reach a judgment as to whether the investment manager's results were due to management skill or merely to good (or bad) luck. The ongoing results of performance evaluation are important because they will determine whether the investment manager will be retained or fired, the amount of the fund's assets the manager will manage, and whether more stringent (or different) guidelines are appropriate.

To assist the pension fund decision makers in this process, the pension fund's staff normally uses a variety of different performance measurement techniques. These techniques range from the highly sophisticated to the straightforward. For example, one of the more sophisticated performance evaluation techniques allocates performance return into components intended to reflect an investment manager's investment philosophy, security selections, and market timing decisions. A statistical estimate of skill is then made, based on the returns achieved relative to the risk taken over the period in which the returns were measured.

A more straightforward way to measure performance is to construct a benchmark portfolio. A benchmark portfolio attempts to identify the returns from a specific universe within which the investment manager makes security selections. For example, a growth stock benchmark portfolio would be constructed to measure a growth stock manager; a "value" stock benchmark portfolio for a "value" manager; and so forth. This is an attempt to compare an investment manager's stock selection and portfolio construction skills against individual, customized benchmarks.

Yet another way to measure an investment manager's performance is to see how other managers with a similar style have performed during the period in question. These are peer group analyses. For example, a growth stock investment manager would be compared against a group of other growth stock investment managers, and so forth.

A more straightforward approach is to simply measure the manager's performance against some broad market index like the S&P 500. Pension funds normally do not use the Dow Jones Industrial Average as a market benchmark because it does not accurately reflect broad market performance. It contains only 30 stocks and is computed in such a way that biases are introduced.

Each performance measurement system has its pros and cons, but like the decision to hire the manager in the first place, the decision to retain a specific investment manager is also subjective. Historical data is looked at and analyzed, but who is to say that the past will be repeated? In addition, a determined chief investment officer can assemble "facts" to "prove" just about anything he or she wants to about a specific investment manager. Finally, a "friendly" consultant can add credibility to the decision and thus give comfort to any committee. It is simply too easy for a chief investment officer to hide a personal agenda from view.

PENSION FUND PERFORMANCE REVIEW

It is very important to measure the chief investment officer's performance results. A skillful person can make a difference to the company and to the plan participants, and so can having a bad one.

Not too surprisingly, the system for analyzing a chief investment officer's decisions is not as well developed as that for evaluating investment managers. The chief investment officer wants to keep his or her job. It is more convenient to prove that an investment manager, or a member of the pension fund's staff, should be fired instead.

One way to measure the value a chief investment officer added to the pension fund is to construct a benchmark using the pension fund's normal asset mix. The mechanics are straightforward. At the end of each year, multiply the performance of an index which is representative of the performance of that investment type by the category's percentage in the normal asset mix. Do this for each of the investment categories in the pension fund and add up the resulting values. Now compare that total to the end of the year performance achieved by the fund. This measure provides an indication as to how well in aggregate a chief investment officer has done in selecting investment managers and in allocating assets. It's not the total picture because it doesn't measure the decision-making process in constructing the normal asset mix, but it does give an indication of a chief investment officer's skill in key areas under his or her control.

Another approach is peer review — seeing how well one pension fund performed relative to other pension funds with similar objectives. It's not easy getting the comparisons though. Many chief investment officers simply don't want to share their performance results. They do not want to be measured. It is as simple as that.

One independent source of peer group performance numbers, however, comes from the Trust Universe Comparison System (TUCS). This is a group of master trustees who supply information on pension fund performance via a consultant. Some of the possible pension fund comparisons are "All Master Trusts," "All Corporate Master Trusts," "Corporate Master Trusts greater than $1.0 billion in size," and "All Master Trusts greater than $1.0 billion in size."

The critical issue for anyone using TUCS numbers is whether the pension funds included in the index are similar in size, composition, objectives, and restrictions to the pension fund that is being measured. For example, some of the composite indexes include public pension funds, which may have legally imposed investment restrictions. It would not be reasonable to compare a private pension fund, which has no such restrictions, to this index.

Annual data should be used with caution. Unusual circumstances could have produced favorable or unfavorable results. Sometimes investment decisions take several years to work the way they were intended. A moving three- to five-year average of the annual data might provide a more accurate picture of a chief investment officer's skill, or lack thereof. If the return achieved by the fund is substantially less than these benchmarks, watch out. It is not a good sign, and it should raise a lot of questions that should be answered by the current decision makers. If this shortfall continues year after year, a change in decision makers might be warranted.

SUMMARY

A lot of material has been covered in this chapter so a brief recap might be useful. The first and single most important decision made in a pension fund is which types of investment to invest in and how much of the pension fund's money should be allocated to each. Studies have shown this "asset mix" decision explains more than 80 percent of your pension fund's total return.

Next, an investment strategy should be developed for each investment type. The investment strategy should take into account market realities and possibilities. In terms of impact on a pension fund's total return, this is the next most important decision.

Next, competent investment managers, who actually will do the buying and selling of securities, are sought out and hired. Remember, regardless what spin the pension fund decision makers may put on it, selection, and retention, of an investment manager is a subjective decision.

Next, guidelines are established. These are mutually agreed upon statements of investment objectives, style, risk, and performance. They also should address ethical standards.

Finally, performance is monitored. There are some very straightforward methods as well as some more sophisticated approaches. Not only should the investment manager's performance be evaluated, but that of the chief investment officer as well.

APPENDIX 1

Selected Building Blocks for Investment Strategies

I. Common Stocks
    A. Passive Management
        1. S&P 500 Index Fund
        2. Extended Index Fund
        3. Custom Index Funds
    B. Active Management
        1. Market Timing
        2. Sector/Industry Rotation
        3. Growth Stocks
        4. Value Stocks
        5. Yield Stocks
        6. Themes
        7. Large-/Small-Capitalization Stocks
        8. Top Down/Bottom Up

II. Bonds
    A. Passive Management
        1. Index Funds
        2. Immunized Portfolios
        3. Contingent Immunized Portfolios
        4. Laddered Maturities
    B. Active Management
        1. Interest Rate Anticipation
        2. Security Selection
            a) Substitution Swaps
            b) Intermarket Swaps
            c) Pure Yield Pick-up Swaps
            d) Private Placements

III. Real Estate
    A. Direct Ownership
    B. Partnerships/Joint Ventures
    C. Property Types
        1. Retail
        2. Office

          3. Residential/Apartments
          4. Land
     D. Existing/Development
     E. Real Estate Investment Trusts
     F. Mortgages
          1. Mortgage-Backed Securities
          2. Pass Throughs
IV. International
     A. Country Selection
     B. Currency Overlay
     C. Sector/Industry Rotation
     D. Growth Stocks
     E. Value Stocks
     F. Yield Stocks
     G. Themes
     H. Large-/Small-Capitalization Stocks
     I. Top Down/Bottom Up
     J. Index Funds
     K. Emerging Markets
V. Venture Capital
     A. Seed
     B. Early Stage
     C. Mezzanine
     D. Later Stage
     E. Direct/Partnerships
     F. Industry Specific/Eclectic

APPENDIX 2

Investment Strategy — Common Stocks

BACKGROUND

Efficient market theory indicates that, on average, there is no additional reward for assuming nonmarket risk. That being the case, the most effective course of action would be to index 100 percent of the assets allocated to common stock investments. On the other hand, the efficient market theory is just that, a theory. The risk-adjusted performance of some managers has exceeded the market during some time frame.

A compromise position, one that takes into account the theory as well as our expectations for higher than market performance from some managers, has been adopted. The strategy is to index a portion of the funds and to leave the balance to competent active managers. The active managers will be selected and grouped into three style categories. Low-cost diversification is then provided by passive index fund management, and increased concentration and superior returns are expected from the higher cost active managers. Inherent in this strategy is a recognition that the risk and return characteristics of the individual managers are important only as they relate to the aggregate. The process is managed, in part, via the use of risk and return guidelines agreed to in advance with each investment manager.

Flexibility to take advantage of changing market conditions will be provided by the index fund. Assets will be shifted into and out of the index fund to reflect expected future stock market conditions. In addition, core portfolios designed to approximate the risk and return characteristics of two of the three investment style categories will be established. This will facilitate changes in the fund's investment style exposure to take advantage of expected market conditions without disrupting the active managers' investment strategies. The index fund and the two core portfolios will be managed in-house to facilitate this process.

PASSIVE MANAGEMENT

The portion allocated to passive management will depend upon the perception of the likelihood of better than market performance from the active managers, the level of risk assumed by the active managers, the fund's exposure to common stocks, and the acceptable level of risk for the stock portion of the fund. These interrelated factors will be subjected to periodic review. Asset allocation models, optimization techniques, manager performance analyses, and market expectations will provide the basic input to the decision-making process.

ACTIVE MANAGEMENT

Correlation analyses indicated that three very broad groupings of investment management styles appear appropriate. These are growth stocks, value stocks, and styles that cannot be classified as either. Within these groupings, subcategorizations are important. By retaining style groupings that are lowly correlated, the fund will be able to change its nonmarket exposure by varying its exposure to those styles. Emphasizing stock selection within the style categories should cause the composition of nonmarket risk to emphasize the specific risk component. Thus, the objective is to provide the opportunity to adjust for expected style performance, but at the same time to increase exposure to the active manager's stock selection capabilities.

The number of active managers will be limited. First, the more active managers in the pension fund the more the aggregate will resemble a big, high-cost index fund. Second, limiting the number of active managers imposes a discipline on the fund to keep only the best ones. Finally, the fewer the number of active managers, the lower the pension fund's administrative costs.

Within stylistic constraints, each manager's portfolio size generally will be limited to $200 to 300 million. Limiting portfolio size should allow the manager to more fully reflect his best investment ideas in the portfolio and for those ideas to be reflected in the pension fund's common stock return. If the active manager's account is at maximum, growth in pension fund assets will be accommodated through expansion of passive management.

NORMAL MIX

It is expected that over a 5- to 10-year horizon the pension fund's common stock exposure will have the following mix:

	Percent of common stock assets	Percent of investment style
Passive management	40%	—
Active management	60%	
Growth stocks		40%
Value stocks		40%
Other styles		20%
	100%	100%

PERFORMANCE

The pension fund's common stock investments will be measured over a rolling three- to five-year period. In evaluating performance, consideration will be given to the investment market conditions during the period and the level of risk taken. In general, the fund's common stock investments, in aggregate and adjusted for management fees, are expected to exceed:

a. The average rate of return from an outside S&P 500 index fund.

b. The average rate of return of the common stock investments of other comparable pension funds.

c. The average rate of return of common stock mutual funds.

d. The average rate of return of a benchmark calculated using the normal mix above and the average rate of return from stylistically similar Lipper indices.

CHAPTER 5

Who Runs the Pension Fund?

This chapter provides an overview of the organizations involved in managing a pension fund for a corporate defined benefit plan. But more than that, it gives the reader a feel for the pressures placed on the individuals in those organizations, because it is within the mosaic of politics and personalities that choices are shaped and decisions are made.

ORGANIZATION CHART

Certain individuals are given the responsibility for overseeing the investment of the money accumulated in the pension fund. These individuals are known by various titles and descriptions, but generally are considered trustees. They have certain fiduciary responsibilities to see that the money in the pension fund is invested in the sole interest of plan participants.

In a corporate pension fund this responsibility lies with certain members of the board of directors. Often, however, they will delegate that responsibility to others, so the definition of a fiduciary of a company's pension fund includes officers and directors of the plan, members of the investment committees, investment managers, and persons who select those individuals. In legal terms a fiduciary is someone who has a very high duty of care in his or her dealings with another's assets.

FIGURE 5–1

Sample Organization Structure

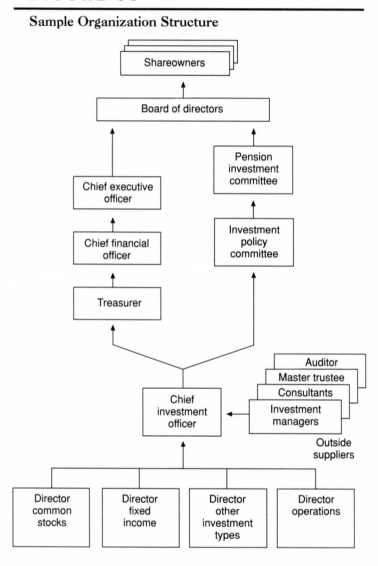

Figure 5–1 is representative of how the people who manage a corporate pension fund are typically organized.

While this organization looks straightforward on paper, with each role clearly defined, reality can be something else. It may be through lethargy, a lack of "street smarts," greed for increased fees by outside suppliers, and/or fear of losing one's job that the entire process can be controlled by just a few individuals. When combined with a lack of proper controls, this becomes a perfect environment for fraud and wrongdoing to run rampant.

BOARD OF DIRECTORS

The board of directors, normally a small group of not more than 20 or so individuals, is elected by the shareowners of the company. The shareowners own the company, and the board must report to them. Individual shareowners might not realize this because the number of shares they own is probably small relative to the total number of shares outstanding for the company. Nevertheless, they do own a fraction of the company, and, collectively with other shareowners, they own the entire company. Many pension plan participants are also shareowners, and, collectively, they too own a portion of the company. This gives plan participants and retirees some leverage over the selection of board members, if they choose to use it.

The board of directors plays a very important role in the functioning of a firm. It normally establishes corporate policies, provides high-level counsel, reviews performance, and makes changes in strategic direction. Finally, and most importantly, the board's key job is to hire, fire, and compensate the chief executive officer. The chief executive officer is the highest ranking employee in the company and reports to the board of directors.

The board is supposed to take actions that are in the best interests of shareowners after, in the author's opinion, giving due consideration to its customers, employees, and retirees. Although the day-to-day operating responsibilities are generally left up to senior management, the board is kept informed by various reports and presentations made to it. If it chooses, it can look into whatever business affairs of the company it wants, ask questions of any employee, and hire various consultants or agents to help it execute its duties and responsibilities.

The chief executive officer, in turn, selects other senior managers to help him or her run the company. They, in turn, select other individuals, and so forth throughout the organization.

So the chief executive officer reports and is accountable to the board of directors which, in turn, reports and is accountable to the shareowners. At least that is the way it is supposed to work. Reality is sometimes different. Let's start with the board's control over the chief executive officer. Sadly, some senior executives seem to control their boards, rather than the other way around. Indeed, in one of his funnier quips, Ross Perot allegedly called GM's board of directors management's "pet rocks." (To be fair, GM's board has recently taken, what is for corporate America, some aggressive actions to exert more control over the company's management.)

If the chief executive officer controls the board rather than the other way around, the company risks becoming the chief executive officer's private fiefdom. Decisions brought to the board will be rubber stamped, senior management compensation and perks get out of hand, and self-interest takes over. This could even extend to the chief executive officer using the pension fund and its resources to advance corporate or personal goals.

At first it might seem impossible for a chief executive officer to exercise control over a board of directors and the trustees of the pension fund, given that the shareowners elect board members. However, to repeat a remark attributed to Congressman John Dingell of Michigan: "If you let me write procedure and I let you write substance, I'll screw you every time."[1]

He reportedly was referring to getting a bill through Congress, but he might as well have been referring to the procedures a company might have for the election of directors — election rules the former Soviet Union would be proud of.

Consider this. First, the board determines the qualifications for membership and develops a list of who should fill any openings. It should not be a surprise that existing board members might tend to pick people who think like themselves. Moreover, it is doubtful that the list would not have been at least "reviewed" with the chief executive officer before it was finalized.

Second, the company uses its own money and resources to prepare and to send to each of its shareowners the list of candidates that the board has selected to fill open spots. If someone wants to propose another list of candidates, and they make their way through a labyrinth of election rules and procedures, they must incur the cost of

---

1. "Of Filibusters and House Rules — Controlling Procedures Means Control of Policies," *Investors Business Daily*, August 16, 1994.

communicating with shareowners themselves. If the company has tens of thousands of shareowners, this could be a very expensive proposition.

Third, voting one's shares can be confusing — not so much which box to check but understanding the issues involved. Each year before a company's annual meeting, shareowners receive a proxy statement. Some of them might simply toss this material into the bin or check the box for management, including the individuals the company wants to fill open board spots, without reading or understanding all the issues. Many shareowners have no desire to get involved in managing a company. They became shareowners because they thought they could make some money. If they now don't like the direction the company is headed it is easier for them to sell the stock and buy something else. (Institutional shareowners are becoming more active in the affairs of corporations in which they own large blocks of shares, but they are looking out after their own interests, which may or may not coincide with the interests of pension plan participants.)

Finally, some companies have rules whereby the directors serve staggered terms, so perhaps only a third of the board members come up for election each year. Thus, in any given year no outside group can gain control of the board.

Directors are typically identified as either inside or outside directors. An employee who gets elected to the board is called an inside director. Since employees report to the chief executive officer, they can be the easiest directors to control. A board stacked with insiders gives the chief executive officer a powerful edge.

Outside directors — individuals who are not employees of the company — require a carrot rather than the stick of fear used on inside directors. A chief executive officer has many carrots — high director fees, consulting contracts, and/or other company business. These might make an outside director more willing to "appreciate" the chief executive's point of view when decisions are made.

> The fact is, most chief executives wield enormous leverage over the board. For one thing, boards don't like to overrule the chief executive, who is usually also the chairman of the board. For another, it's the chief executive officer who has a significant say in nominating directors. Three years ago William Glavin, president of Babson College and a director of several corporations, sat on the board of a midsize

company; Glavin declines to identify the company. Glavin questioned the chairman's decision on his retirement plans, and consequently the chairman, miffed, asked Glavin to leave.

At first Glavin agreed to go quietly. Then he learned the chairman was telling other directors he was making a be-on-my-side-or-be-gone example of Glavin. Furious, Glavin then planned to take his ouster before the entire board. Though he felt he had enough board support, Glavin decided to resign anyway, citing "personal reasons."

Chief executives who don't want to directly confront an unwanted board member can always try the "freeze-out" method. Arnold Ross, president of New York compensation consulting firm Hirschfeld, Stern, Moyer & Ross, explains how that worked in one recent case. A company's chairman first took away a director's $100,000-a-year job as a public relations and marketing consultant, then removed him from the board's audit and nominating committees. The director then got the snub from fellow board members, who didn't invite him to dinner meetings and in one case even refused to sit next to him at lunch. After several months of this schoolyard treatment, the director finally got the hint and sullenly resigned.

The article ends with this sentence:

In most board member disputes, the boss [the chief executive officer] has the last laugh.[2]

If you're thinking that's an isolated example, consider this:

[Retired chief executive officer of Monsanto, John Hanley, accepted an invitation from a chief executive officer] to join his board — subject, Hanley wrote, to meeting with the company's general counsel and outside accountants as a kind of directorial due diligence. Says Hanley: "At the first board dinner the CEO got up and said, 'I think Jack was a little bit confused whether we wanted him to be a director or the chief executive officer.' I should have known right there that he wasn't going to pay a goddamn bit of attention to anything I said." So it turned out, and after a year Hanley quit the board in disgust.[3]

The board of directors is supposed to rein all this in and keep the company on track. But even the most conscientious and independent director faces a tough job. First, consider the flow of information.

---

2. "Operation Deadwood," *Forbes*, May 21, 1993.

3. "Reviving Internal Corporate Control Systems," Presidential address by Michael C. Jensen, delivered to the American Finance Association, 1992.

Often any information the board gets comes from the company via the chief executive officer's desk. Even the board meeting agenda could be prepared by the chief executive officer. Control the flow of information and you can control the decisions.

Next, some boards are just too large to function effectively. With a large board it is often easier for a chief executive officer to influence outcomes.

Third, potential legal liability may cause board members to avoid taking independent action. It might be safer to delegate responsibilities to senior management or seek massive protections from the company. Some companies do a pretty good job of protecting their directors from the consequences of their decisions. Consider the scope of a blanket indemnification one company proposed to give its directors. This is what that company said in its proxy statement if the proposal was approved by shareowners:

> Directors will no longer be liable for monetary damages based on breach of the duty or care even if the breach involved negligence or *gross negligence* . . . [Emphasis added.]

The company might argue that without these protections no one would want to be a director. Perhaps. But all these protections could influence the due diligence a director is supposed to exercise when making a decision.

A fourth factor is lack of time. In addition to being high-ranking executives in their own companies, many directors serve on several other boards and community committees.

Finally, a director who is being well treated might be more appreciative of the chief executive officer's viewpoint. How much do directors get paid? It varies, but take this one example from a company's proxy statement. Outside directors (individuals who are not employees) receive an annual retainer of $41,000. They also receive an additional annual retainer of $5,000 for each active committee on which they serve; $6,000 goes to anyone who becomes a chairman of the committee. (The board of directors often establishes committees that have responsibilities for specific functions — more about this later.)

And that's not all. Nonemployee directors at this company also participate in a "retirement" plan and are given 1,500 shares of the company's common stock after each annual meeting, at which directors are elected. At today's stock price that retirement grant is worth $60,000. But wait, there is even more: Each grant is accompanied by an additional payment to offset the increase in the director's federal, state, and local taxes. So the $60,000 grant is tax free. In before tax dollars the grant is worth about $100,000. Add to that the $41,000 retainer, and another $5,000 ($6,000 if serving on a committee as its chairman), and total annual income of a director in this company becomes about $145,000. This does not even count the opportunity for lucrative "consulting" contracts.

Consulting contracts with board members at one company ranged from $85,000 for advice on overseas business opportunities to $585,000 for counsel on pension investment matters. What's more, two of these company's directors had severance agreements included in their consultantships. If the company were to change hands and they lost their consulting arrangements they were to be paid 2.99 times their average fee for the last five years — sort of a golden parachute for director-consultants.[4]

In short, the benefits of being on the board of directors can be substantial. And not everything is necessarily reported to the shareowners:

> Directors earn much more in benefits than shareholders think. Board compensation runs at least 50% more than proxies indicate, once the real dollar value of benefits is counted, says Robert Stobaugh, a Harvard Business School professor . . . "For every dollar you read about in the proxy, there's another 62 cents that goes unvalued," he says.[5]

At least shareowners have an option. If they become disgusted with an overpaid or docile board or with the way senior executives are running the company, they can always sell their stock. Ditto for employees — they too have a choice; they could leave.

How about retirees? What choices do they have? The sad truth is that retirees and other pension plan participants are stuck. They can't leave the pension fund. They are locked in and are dependent upon whatever is dictated to them by the company. Often they do not have a voice in the affairs of the pension fund and they are kept in the dark about what is going on. This must change.

---

4. "Double Duty: Board Outsider, Paid Consultant," *The Wall Street Journal*, March 17, 1995.
5. "Business Bulletin," *The Wall Street Journal*, January 5, 1995.

PENSION INVESTMENT COMMITTEE

The board of directors often sets up a committee composed of board members to help oversee the pension fund's investment activities. The name of this committee varies, and sometimes its functions are included with other committees. This book assumes only one committee has this responsibility and calls it the pension investment committee. Who sits on it, as well as who chairs the committee and how often it meets, is up to the board of directors. These individuals are normally thought of as the pension plan's trustees.

The responsibilities of the pension investment committee vary from company to company. Typically, they include overseeing the investment of pension fund assets, establishing investment policies, approving investment managers for the plans, and reviewing the performance of the managers and plan assets.

As stated earlier, the members of this board committee often delegate responsibilities to company employees. When such delegation occurs, the pension investment committee takes on an advisory role, with the real decisions being made at the lower level. If wrongdoing hits the fan, the following legal argument is then used:

> Whether Union Carbide's, or any other pension fund's fiduciaries would have any liability in a pension fraud case would depend upon the fiduciaries' actions in monitoring and appointing its pension executives . . . Just because criminal actions may have take place in the management of a pension plan does not mean any fiduciary liability exists, . . . One would have to ask, "Were they prudent in their methodologies for monitoring their people?"[6]

As noted, committee members typically are very busy individuals. They may welcome the opportunity to delegate their trustee responsibilities to company employees.

INVESTMENT POLICY COMMITTEE

To assume the pension fund investment responsibilities delegated by the board members, the company will typically establish a committee of senior executives, called the investment policy committee. Its responsibilities vary from company to company, but normally include

---

6. "Former Union Carbide Exec Indicted," *Pension & Investments*, September 6, 1993.

such tasks as establishing the normal asset mix; changing the actual asset mix within the specified ranges; hiring and firing investment managers, consultants and trustees; establishing recordkeeping and other administrative standards; approving and monitoring the pension fund's expense budgets; assessing the performance of the chief investment officer and staff; ensuring compliance with various governmental regulations and reports; and establishing the ethical framework within which the fund and all its related personnel operate.

Some very senior corporate executives often serve on this committee. The committee meets periodically during the year, sometimes as often as monthly, but more likely four to five times a year.

Like it or not, politics and corporate culture can exert a strong influence over the group dynamics of this committee and, unfortunately, over the decisions it makes. The committee often includes a very senior person, perhaps even the vice chairmen of the company. This person, because of his or her position, can exert a strong influence on the careers, assignments, and reputations of the other committee members — and the other members know it. Ideally, all of the members should be considered equal. They should be able to express their own views without fear of jeopardizing their careers in the company. The reality, however, is that committee members may be unwilling to sacrifice their corporate ambitions in an argument over an investment decision in the pension.

Another reality is that committee members simply may not have any pension fund investment background. To be fair, committee members may be very knowledgeable about their primary job — running the company. Clearly, they have achieved a measure of success by virtue of their positions. Nevertheless, it does take some specialized skills and pension fund "street smarts" to be an effective member. Some committee members may be simply too busy or too preoccupied with running the business to learn them.

This is a perfect environment for self-serving employees. If committee members are already predisposed to delegate responsibility even further downward, and if those employees can use pension fund suppliers to provide positive feedback, especially to the most senior executive on the committee, getting and controlling the decision-making process can be fairly straightforward. The investment policy committee could easily be turned into a rubber stamp. Even that might be acceptable if the committee sets up the necessary checks and balances and requires strict auditing control. However, a 100 percent delegation of authority to the chief investment officer without the necessary safeguards is foolish.

CHIEF INVESTMENT OFFICER

Again, organizations vary, but because the title of chief investment officer is the most descriptive of the duties of the person who is assigned the responsibility of overseeing the day-to-day investment activities of the pension fund, it will be used in this book.

In addition to the responsibilities delegated to the chief investment officer by the investment policy committee, this person generally has the responsibility of conducting asset allocation studies; identifying the impact alternative asset mixes would have on expected risk and return; developing alternative investment strategies; searching out and evaluating investment managers, consultants, actuaries, and trustees; measuring and evaluating performance results; and recommending changes as required.

Normally, the chief investment officer would report to the chief financial officer or the treasurer of the company so as to fix a spot for the individual within the corporate hierarchy for pay and supervision purposes. The chief investment officer would also be a member of the internal investment policy committee and might even give periodic reports to the board of director's pension investment committee.

The chief investment officer can be a very important linchpin in the entire investment decision-making process. Conceivably, all of the information about the pension fund, its investments, its managers, and its pension fund staff could be provided by the chief investment officer. This includes establishing the investment policy committee meeting agendas, designing reports, orchestrating presentations, and preparing performance results.

STAFF

Typically, the chief investment officer has a staff to help him or her with the detailed work. Staff size often depends on the size and complexity of the pension fund, its investment philosophy, and the talents of the individuals doing the work. Generally, the larger the pension fund, the larger the staff.

The investment management staff should not be confused with the benefits department within the company. Typically, the benefits department administers the pension plan. Most plan participants are familiar with this department, as it is the group they would call with questions about their pension benefits. The investment staff, on the other hand, focuses on investing the assets in the pension fund.

Investment management staff functions are often divided into two parts — investments and operations. Investments deals with providing studies, evaluations, and recommendations relating to establishing the appropriate asset mix, ranges, investment strategies, investment managers, and review processes for the assets in the pension fund. Operations deals with maintaining investment records, acting as the liaison with the plan's actuaries and master trustee, verifying fees, tracking expenses, and maintaining the investment management group's files.

For very large pension funds, specialization within these areas can occur. For example, the investment side might be further divided into more specific functions, with one person having responsibility for common stock investments, another for bonds, and so forth.

Just like the chief investment officer, who is selected by even higher management, the chief investment officer selects his or her staff. As a result, the chief investment officer obviously wields a great deal of power over the careers of staff members.

A host of outside organizations are involved in the pension fund investment process. These include investment managers, consultants, the master trustee, and the plan's actuary. They are the subject of the next four sections.

INVESTMENT MANAGERS

The chief investment officer is sometimes given the responsibility to hire outside investment managers to invest certain portions of the pension fund's assets. These investment managers become fiduciaries for that portion of the fund for which they are responsible.

Duties of an investment manager vary, but often include identifying securities and investments that are expected to provide the optimal risk/return tradeoff; determining the appropriate time to buy and sell specific securities and other investments; determining and maintaining the concentration of assets in specific securities such that the risk/return characteristics of the portfolio are optimized; following investment guidelines established by the chief investment officer; and providing periodic updates of performance results and strategies.

Investment management can also be provided by the pension fund staff itself. This is called internal or inside management. The responsibilities and reporting requirements of inside investment managers should be the same as for outside managers.

CONSULTANTS

Usually a chief investment officer hires a consultant for projects he or she feels staff can't handle either because of the specialized nature of the project or because of time constraints. Realistically, however, consultants can also be hired to give credibility to a decision the chief investment officer has already made. It is human nature for an investment policy committee to obtain a sense of comfort from knowing that a supposedly independent consultant reviewed a decision and agreed with the conclusions. Committee members might accept this "expert" opinion without question and without a thought as to who hired the consultant in the first place.

Projects assigned to a consultant can be grouped into two broad categories: (1) special studies, such as the evaluation of pension fund methods and procedures, reviews and audits of pension fund expenses, assisting with investment manager selection, and assessment of long-term investment policy and strategies; and (2) ongoing evaluations, such as performance measurement, trading evaluations, establishing and maintaining unique benchmarks, monitoring investment managers, and any other functions the pension fund determines can be provided at less cost by a consultant than by staff.

MASTER TRUSTEE

Although various committees, the chief investment officer, and the investment managers are responsible for deciding how the pension assets are to be invested, another trustee typically has custody of the documents of ownership. The trustee is usually a bank, which administers the pension fund's investment activities. This trustee — called a master trustee if it handles all or most of the administrative duties — is responsible for the receipt and disbursement of money, securities and other assets; recording financial transactions; reporting activities, including preparation of various government reports; maintaining records and accounts for benefit recipients; and issuing retirement checks. The master trustee carries out its responsibilities in accordance with a trust agreement.

Rules and procedures identifying the company employees who are authorized to execute transactions on behalf of the pension fund are supposed to be well-documented and faithfully followed by the master trustee. Written instructions establishing the investment manager's role, as well as buy/sell instructions from the investment manager and confirmations from the brokers, are to be kept on file. All of this is intended to provide an audit trail of who has authority to do what and what has happened, when, and at what price.

ACTUARY

An actuarial firm is hired to provide very specialized studies and reports. Its responsibilities typically include providing annual plan valuations to establish plan costs and required contributions; assessing the plan's funded status; developing actuarial information for disclosure purposes; preparing the annual actuarial report for the IRS and appropriate certifications to demonstrate that the plan meets IRS minimum funding standards; preparing actuarial reports for asset and liability transfers and/or plan termination calculations; analyzing the economic and demographic experience of the plan; establishing and documenting actuarial assumptions and methods; and assisting senior executives with understanding the financial implications of possible plan design changes, demographic changes, and acquisitions or divestitures.

CHAPTER 6

Cost to Manage the Fund

A lot of money can be spent running a pension fund — millions in investment management, consulting, brokerage, and other fees for a large pension fund. Think about it. A chief investment officer could have within his or her control the ability to award contracts, pay fees, and make expenditures totaling millions of dollars a year. That's power — the power a chief investment officer can use to get his or her back scratched.

This chapter will illustrate how lucrative the pension fund investment business can be.

INVESTMENT MANAGEMENT FEES

There are many different types of fee arrangements — too many to discuss here. Most, however, are so-called "asset-based" arrangements, where the fee is determined by the amount of assets a pension fund has entrusted to the investment manager. The fee is quoted as a percentage, which generally declines with increasing increments of assets under management. One has to multiply the quoted percentage by the amount of pension fund assets entrusted to the manager to determine the dollar amount of the fee.

Asset-based fee arrangements have a unique characteristic. Because the fee is based on a percentage of assets, as the assets in the account increase with good performance, so does the amount paid to the investment manager. That's fine as long as the investment manager is the one who is responsible for the good performance; however, that is not always the case. For example, in bull markets, such as in the stock and bond markets since 1982, most securities increased in price. Even a randomly selected portfolio of stocks increased in value over this time period. As the markets went up, so did the investment manager's income, without him or her adding any value. They were just lucky enough to be in the right profession at the right time.

Some firms were even motivated to become what is called in the industry "closet indexers." These investment managers would diversify their portfolios so that they would resemble the stock market in general. Because the portfolio would mimic market movements, the manager could be reasonably assured that the performance of the portfolio would be close to that for the market and this, in turn, reduced the likelihood that he or she would be fired for poor performance. Then, as the market went up, so would the investment manager's income.

The past decade or so has been a wonderful environment for many investment management firms. The only real skills required were to get hired in the first place, remain fully invested in a well-diversified portfolio, and not get fired. Investment management was a money-making machine as long as the manager could keep the chief investment officer happy.

Incentive fees have been used from time to time. The structure of these vary widely, but all make some attempt to compensate the investment manager for the good performance that was attributable to the manager's skills. While incentive fee arrangements have appeal, if a pension fund does not carefully monitor a manager's activity, the fee arrangement provides an incentive for the manager to increase the level of risk in the portfolio in order to gain a better shot at higher returns.

How much an investment manager charges for his or her services depends on a number of factors, including the type of investment category and the manager's investment style. For example:

1. Common stock investment managers will typically charge an annual fee between 0.1 and 1.25 percent of the assets in the account per year, depending upon the type of investment style.

2. Bond manager fees are generally lower and, depending upon the type of investment style, typically range between 0.1 and 0.5 percent of the assets in the account per year.

3. Venture capital fees range all over the place. The most typical fees are 2.5 percent of the assets in the account per year and 20 percent of any of the profits made on the transactions.

4. Real estate fees are something else again. When all the managing, leasing, purchasing, and selling fees are totaled and amortized, real estate fees can be 2 to 5 percent of the net asset value of the property each year.

To get a better feel for the magnitude of the fees, these percentages will be converted into dollars using common stock investments as an example. Later, since they are unique, venture capital and real estate fees will be explored in depth.

First, consider the different types of common stock investment styles since different styles generally have different fee levels. So-called "passive" investment management styles, for example, have lower fees because they are easier and less costly to implement. As indicated earlier, "passive" management replicates the risk and return characteristics of a stock market index without attempting to determine which investments within that index might outperform the others.

Since passive management is relatively straightforward, the management fee charged for the service by investment managers is relatively low, say 0.1 percent of the assets under management per year. For a $300 million account, that would mean a $300,000 annual fee. Now, $300,000 a year is a lot of money, but just wait. The size of investment management fees gets even larger as discretionary investment judgment enters into the investment process. That's called "active" management.

In active management, the other major grouping of investment style, a manager would screen through hundreds and hundreds of stocks and invest only in those he or she considered to be the very best. Unlike a passive manager, who might have 500 or more stocks in a portfolio, an active manager's portfolio may contain only 30 to 50 stocks. The hope is the investment manager has indeed picked the best stocks and the portfolio will outperform the return provided by passive management.

For this service, the active manager charges a higher fee — say 0.5 percent of the assets under management. If our active manager had the same $300 million account, the fees paid by the pension fund to the outside investment manager would be $1.5 million a year.

$1.5 million a year in fees is not too shabby from the investment manager's viewpoint — but wait, there's more. Because of the nature of the business, fixed costs (office space, computers, salaries, databases, etc.) are relatively small. Once those costs are covered, all the remaining revenue flows directly into the pockets of the owners. Adding another account typically does not increase expenses significantly. Upwards of 70 percent of new account's revenue can be pure profit. Continuing with our example, that could mean a new pension fund account could be worth 70 percent of $1.5 million, or more than $1 million a year in profit to the owners of the investment management firm.

There is even more.

Typically, a pension fund decision maker would be very reluctant to fire a newly hired manager. The decision maker would have to admit he or she made a mistake and psychologically that is very hard for some people to do. Normally, an investment manager is given 3 to 5 years to "prove" himself or herself. So, 3 to 5 years at $1 million a year in profit means that signing up a pension fund really is worth $3 to 5 million to the owners of the investment management firm.

Wait, there is *still* more!

The author has seen the fortunes of investment management firms literally turn around when a large pension fund signed on as a client. Often, there is a coat-tail effect. When a big, influential pension fund hires an investment manager, other pension funds figure this manager must be all right. The odds of the investment management firm adding more new accounts improve. Therefore, not only is a new pension fund account with a major pension worth $3 to 5 million to the owners of the investment management firm over the expected minimum life of the contract, but it is potentially worth much more as the investment manager uses the pension fund's name to market its services to other pension funds and investors.

Senior-level partners at large investment management firms can earn $10 to $15 million a year in cash compensation, not including options or equity participation. And in case there was any doubt about who is most important to a firm's financial success — a portfolio manager who makes the investment decisions or a marketing manager who brings in the accounts — consider this: The average compensation, including bonus, was $211,000 a year for marketing professionals versus $210,000 for portfolio managers.[1]

> "People that are bringing in business are getting more bang for their buck . . . Anybody who can bring in the business is really cherished," Mr. Burkhart [president of Investment Counseling] said.[2]

Obviously, smaller accounts generate less money in fees and sometimes are more costly to administer, but the dollars paid in management fees still can be large. And remember, once the investment manager's fixed costs are covered, much of the revenue generated by adding a new account goes right into the pockets of the owners.

Thus, investment management can be very lucrative, but it's also very competitive. Practically anyone who wants to start an investment management business can do so. The "barriers to entry" are low. Office space, computers, databases, telephones, and some operating expenses about cover it as far as costs go. In most unregulated businesses, low barriers to entry, high profit margins, and keen competition often result in the free market forcing profits down, but not in this case.

Because of the huge profit potential and the limited barriers to entry, there are hundreds and hundreds of investment management firms scrambling for business. On a typical day the author would receive three to four calls from investment management firms wanting to sell the pension fund their services. Some firms would even engage in what is called "dialing for dollars." They would get a directory of all the pension funds in the United States and start cold calling to pitch their services.

Given the intense competition for business, it can be extremely cut-throat. In this type of environment some investment managers might be willing to do almost anything to get and keep an account.

CONSULTING FEES

How large can consulting fees get? Try $500,000 a year for a single consulting firm — a sizable chunk of business. And, as is the case with

---

1. "Big Pay Hikes at Money Management Firms," *Pensions & Investments*, April 18, 1994.
2. Ibid.

investment managers, there is some marketing value to having a big pension fund as a client. Fees typically come in two forms: those for ongoing work and those for special projects. Both have high profit margins, but special projects can offer the highest. Sometimes a pension fund puts a specific consultant on a retainer basis; that is, a certain dollar amount is agreed to and the consultant charges special projects against it.

Consultant services are provided by a number of different companies. Some specialize in pension fund work; others, like master trustees (explained in Chapter 5), provide consulting work as a sideline. Fees often are paid in directed brokerage, which will be explained in the next section.

Some consultants are even entering into the investment management business by offering manager-of-managers programs. This is where a consultant seeks out and hires several investment managers and packages them into a sort of mutual fund, which is then made available to predominantly small to medium-sized pension funds. Such a product saves the pension fund from selecting investment managers itself, but presents a potential conflict of interest. The consultant might push its own mutual fund, with its higher fees, rather than just recommending individual managers. Fees for a manager-of-managers mutual fund (also known as a fund-of-funds) can be about 1 percent of the market value of assets under management. This is on top of the fees the investment managers in the fund charge.

DIRECTED BROKERAGE (OR SOFT DOLLAR) AGREEMENTS

Various consulting services can be paid for through directed brokerage agreements. These agreements are also known as "soft dollar" arrangements because the pension fund does not pay with cash, at least not directly. This is how such arrangements generally work. A chief investment officer directs one or more of the pension fund's investment managers, usually common stock managers, to trade securities in the pension fund's account through a specific broker. Typically, the chief investment officer does not demand that all trades be funneled to this broker, just a certain portion or dollar amount.

The broker executes the trades and charges the investment manager a commission to which a few extra cents per share is added and/or a small amount of the increased revenue generated by the additional business directed the broker's way is set aside. These "extras" are accumulated, and the cash generated is then paid to the consultant designated by the chief investment officer.

Use of directed commissions has been hotly debated within the pension fund community. Either way, the pension fund pays the consultant — through cash payments or through the backdoor approach of directed brokerage, though it is difficult to determine which is the least expensive. Second, a consultant who is in a position to recommend investment managers to a pension fund might have as one of its unspoken criteria a requirement that the recommended manager also be willing to direct commissions to the consultant-specified broker. The consultant might reason that having the ability to direct brokerage, plus an investment manager willing to do so, could increase the consultant's pension fund business by giving the chief investment officer an alternate way to pay the consultant's bill. Finally, directed brokerage is sometimes an off-budget item for the chief investment officer. That is, it might not even appear in the list of expenses paid by the pension fund. The question then becomes whether the consultant, or other pension fund supplier who accepts soft dollar payments, is hired because he or she provides the best services or gives the chief investment officer the best freebies.

An investment policy committee that lacks street smarts often does not even know about, much less monitor, these directed brokerage payments. This represents a very convenient way to hide one's activities if the chief investment officer so chooses. The amount a chief investment officer of a large pension fund could have available to compensate consultants and other suppliers for their services using directed brokerage could total over a million dollars a year.

But surely someone must know about it? Of course. Someone on the staff has to handle the paperwork, and the chief investment officer has to ask (order?) an investment manager to direct his or her trades to the specified broker. Some investment managers get upset if they have to direct too many of their trades through a given broker. First, if the specified broker charges too much or is not good at executing trades, the investment manager's portfolio performance can suffer. Second, some investment managers use soft dollars to pay for their own investment research. The more soft dollars that are given to the pension fund, the less are available for the investment manager's use.

A chief investment officer can strong-arm an investment manager into living up to his or her directed brokerage assignment, usually without a threat of being fired. All a chief investment officer has to do is mention the amount of directed brokerage the pension fund has allocated to the investment manager after an "intense" discussion of the investment manager's performance. Whether the investment manager should have been chastised for poor performance does not matter. All that is needed is to plant a seed that the account relationship might be in jeopardy and see how fast an investment manager will catch the hint of the need to live up to his or her directed brokerage assignment.

FINDER FEES

Persons with good contacts within the pension fund community frequently are hired by people who do not have such contacts, and a fee is paid based on the business this individual generates. For example, a venture capital firm might be willing to pay a $90,000 finder's fee to get a $2 million investment commitment from the pension fund. This arrangement is not necessarily wrong or illegal. The venture capital firm, or other firms who pay finder fees, may simply not have the marketing skills necessary to attract pension fund money.

In general, finder fees are one-shot deals. The finder brings in some pension fund business and collects a fee from the investment manager. Some people, however, specialize in putting deals together. They might know many investment managers who would be willing to pay them to get a pension fund account.

One investment manager said his firm stayed away from these people, but was approached from time to time by brokers who had influence with smaller plans and who offered to "deliver the business" if the investment manager gave the broker the commissions on that account.

Permanent employees of an investment management or brokerage firm can also share in quasi-finder fees in that they might receive substantial bonuses for each new pension fund account they sign up. For example, say a brokerage firm acts as an intermediary for a real estate investment manager. If the salesperson is able to get the pen-

sion fund to make, say, a $50 million commitment to a real estate part-
nership, the real estate investment manager might pay the brokerage
firm a 2 percent finder's fee, or $1 million. By prior agreement, the
brokerage firm may split the fee with the salesperson on a 30/70 basis.
In that case, the salesperson would get 30 percent of the $1 million
finder's fee, or $300,000.

Finder fees can also apply to goods and services provided to the
pension fund. Say the finder brings the pension fund a computer ven-
dor who promises to tie all the personal computers together into a
local area network (LAN). For a $100,000 bill it would be reasonable
to expect a $15,000 to $20,000 finder's fee.

The beauty of finder fees is that no one within the pension fund
need know that a fee has been paid. If a venture capital firm does send
a letter outlining the finder fees that were paid, a chief investment officer can simply instruct a subordinate to remove the letter from file
and tell the manager to never write such a letter again.

VENTURE CAPITAL

Venture capital fees typically have an ongoing, annual management
fee and a claim on a percentage of the profits. But that's not all —
many of these agreements say the pension fund cannot terminate the
manager for 10 years. Think about that: A 10-year, no-cut contract,
plus a 2½ percent annual management fee, on top of 20 percent of the
profits (the typical arrangement).

The venture capitalist would argue that appropriate incentives
are necessary to motivate the venture capital firm to do a good job.
Perhaps, but having a guaranteed job for 10 years should be worth
something, too.

Some assumptions are needed to estimate the dollar amount of
the fees. A typical amount of pension fund money given to a venture
capitalist by a large pension fund is about $5 million. So 2½ percent
annually on the $5 million commitment totals $1.25 million over the
10-year life of the agreement.

The real unknown is how much profit the partnership will realize. To get a ballpark idea, assume that when this contract was entered
into, Treasury bonds were providing an 8 percent yield. Although the
venture capitalist would not invest in Treasury bonds, for this example say that the entire $5 million was used to buy these bonds. They

represent the "riskless" return a pension fund could earn over the 10-year investment horizon. In 10 years (the life of the contract), the Treasury bonds would more than double in value. The profits in the deal would be $5 million and the venture capitalist's share would be $1 million ($5 million times 20 percent).

Therefore, over the 10-year life of the agreement, the investment manager would receive $1.25 million in management fees and, at the end of the contract, a lump sum of $1 million. Adding up all the cash flow would mean the total fees paid to this venture capital partnership would be $2.25 million over the life of the contract.

A huge step-up in income potential comes if other pension funds or investors are convinced to join the partnership. This is where the coattail effect of a large pension fund signing on has a great impact. The chief investment officer's real leverage comes when he or she is willing to provide the seed money for a new investment that would never have gotten off the ground without that commitment. For example, if the partnership could raise $70 million from several investors the income over the 10-year period could be a whopping $34 million.

REAL ESTATE

Because of the nature of real estate, the total fees paid to an investment management firm can be substantially more than what appears on the surface. The most visible fee, the investment management fee, is paid to a manager to identify the appropriate property, to negotiate its acquisition, and to provide oversite management once the property is acquired. Oversite management consists of formulating a property management plan, establishing budgets, monitoring expenses, and providing feedback to the pension fund.

The "unseen" fees are for on-site management and negotiating leases. Sometimes a cosubsidiary or affiliate of the investment management firm provides the on-site management and collects the fee. On-site management services include collecting rents, arranging for house services, paying bills, and providing general, day-to-day property management. Finally, a fee is expected for negotiating leases with existing and new tenants. This fee is either paid to another cosubsidiary of the investment management firm or to an outside broker. There is nothing wrong with these fees; they are proper and to be expected.

The investment management fee is typically quoted as an annual percentage applied to some asset base. This asset base can be either the original purchase price of the property, its current market value (the most typical arrangement), or the current equity value of the property (market value minus any mortgages). Like other asset-based fees, if the value of the property increases (say because of inflation), the investment manager's fees will also go up in lockstep, even though that manager added no value.

Assume a pension fund is considering a deal brought to it by a real estate investment manager, involving the acquisition of a $52.6 million shopping center in southern California. Here is an example of the fees a pension fund might be expected to pay:

Investment Management Fee	
1.2% of market value of property	$630,000
On-site Management Fee	
3% of gross revenues	120,000
Leasing Fees	
New leases @ $3 per square foot	
Renewals @ $1,500 per lease	50,000
	$800,000 per year

For each year the pension fund owns the property, the investment manager and its cosubsidiaries, to the extent they provide on-site and leasing services, receive a gross revenue stream of $800,000. As the property's value increases, either through good management, luck, or inflation, so does the manager's revenue stream. In addition, legal expenses, engineering analyses, brokerage fees, closing costs, appraisal fees, survey expenses, accounting expenses, and so on, when applicable, are generally extra and paid by the pension fund or billed back to the tenants.

How long the property would be held is unknown. Even though it may be in the pension fund's best interests to sell a property it owns, the real estate investment manager may be hesitant to make such a recommendation because then the management fees would stop. For sake of example, say the property is sold in eight years. This means getting the pension fund to sign on the dotted line is worth $6.4 million to the investment management firm.

Most real estate investment managers deal with the dilemma of when to sell a property in a professional way. However, senior pension fund executives should be cognizant of this potential conflict and perhaps re-align the fee structure such that both the manager's and the pension fund's interests coincide. Most of the benefits for a real estate manager begin when the client is signed up and the property is purchased. On the other hand, most of the investment return for the pension fund comes when the property is sold. One way to at least partially align the interests is to push back the benefits for the real estate manager. This could involve dividing the flat investment management fee into functions. Under this fee arrangement, a real estate investment manager would receive a fee for identifying and negotiating the purchase of the property, another ongoing fee to oversee its management, and a larger fee when the property is sold. The sales fee could also include a split of the profits above some threshold amount which takes into account increases in property value caused by inflation.

TRADING COSTS

Trading costs — the cost to buy and sell securities — are incurred as a result of the investment decisions of either the investment managers or the pension fund itself. The investment managers buy and sell securities all the time. For example, the turnover rate at which securities are bought and sold in an active common stock portfolio can range from a few percent a year to over 100 percent. The chief investment officer of the pension fund can initiate a huge amount of trading as well. This comes from changes in the asset mix, such as selling international bonds to buy international stocks; changes in investment strategy; and firing and hiring new investment managers. Trading initiated by the chief investment officer could be in the billions of dollars. For example, one pension fund changed its bond investment strategy, fired several investment managers, and hired one manager all in one fell swoop, with one broker executing the transaction. That shift involved several billions of dollars in trades.

The money a brokerage firm makes in executing these trades comes from two sources. The one most people are familiar with is commissions. Commissions are normally quoted as a percentage of the transaction or, more typically for stocks, in cents per share. The second source of income for the broker is from the bid/ask spread — the difference in price between what a broker is willing to pay for a security and what he or she is willing to sell it for. The difference between the two is the additional amount the middleman (the broker) collects for doing the trade.

To get a better feel for the amounts involved, consider an example. Assume a chief investment officer wanted to reduce the pension fund's exposure to common stocks by $500 million. He or she wants to sell stocks and use the proceeds to purchase bonds. How much money could a brokerage firm make out of this transaction?

First, consider the commissions on the sale of the stocks. Say the cost is 3 cents a share and the chief investment officer has 10 million shares to trade in the $500 million sale. That's $300,000 to the brokerage firm. Now assume the spread between what the broker is willing to pay for the shares and what the broker can turn around and sell them for is one-eighth to one-fourth of a point per share. That is about 12.5 to 25 cents per share. Assuming an average of 15 cents a share, that amounts to $1.5 million (15 cents times 10 million shares). Add to that another $300,000 in commissions charged to whoever purchased the shares, and the broker, as a middleman, stands to collect $2.1 million ($300,000 + $1.5 million + $300,000) for selling the stock holdings.

Now consider the cost to purchase the bonds. Normally there is no explicit commission charged on the purchase of bonds. Instead, the broker makes all its money in the bid/ask spread — which can be very large indeed.[3] For our purposes let's just say the bid/ask spread is ½ percent, or $2.5 million.

Adding it all up, the total amount that a broker can collect on this transaction is about $4.6 million. And, as is the case with an investment management firm, once the fixed costs to operate the business — office space, computer systems, and personnel — are covered, any additional revenue goes to the bottom line. In short, a lot of that $4.6 million is profit.

PERSPECTIVE

Nothing in this chapter argues that the decision to hire an investment manager or the decision to trade securities was profitable or unprofitable for the pension fund, whether the estimates of fees paid are too

---

3. See Michael Lewis, *Liars Poker*, Penguin Books, 1989, for an inside look at, among other things, the spreads a broker can collect for trading bonds.

high or too low, or whether the fees charged are truly outrageous. The point is that the pension fund suppliers and the company employees responsible for hiring them both know there is a substantial profit on the table from executing a contract. Most deal with this in a responsible way that is in the best interests of plan participants. Some, however, may decide to take advantage of the situation for personal gain.

Through the use of economic blackmail, it is relatively easy for a chief investment officer to get what he or she wants from a predisposed supplier. Yet it may never dawn on the trustees to ask about fees, despite the fact that fees provide the leverage a chief investment officer needs to "play the game" for personal gain.

CHAPTER 7

A Little Piece
of the Action

Couple a salesperson who is motivated to close a deal any way he or she can with a chief investment officer who wants his or her "back scratched," and a perfect environment for abuse has been created. This chapter outlines some of the "perks" offered by pension fund suppliers.

TEMPTATION

Being a chief investment officer of a large pension fund can be pretty heady stuff. At the stroke of a pen the chief investment officer can easily make someone a millionaire — or take it away just as fast. Given that kind of power, some pension fund suppliers, and those who want to be suppliers, might be willing to do whatever it takes to make, and keep, the chief investment officer happy. It's a competitive world, and literally millions of dollars in fees can be at stake. So the temptation to play the game is strong, especially if the chief investment officer is receptive.

Some pension fund suppliers might pull out all the stops. The chief investment officer will be wined and dined, met at the airport by limousines, whisked to exclusive clubs and private dining rooms, treated with respect almost bordering on reverence, introduced to major players in the political arena, and given the opportunity to hobnob with celebrities. Every major sporting event, sold-out Broadway play, or concert will be made available. Everyone will seem to be the chief investment officer's best friend. It's called sucking up, and the stakes can be big.

Some chief investment officers and lawyers might argue there is nothing wrong with receiving special favors from pension fund suppliers as long as the corporate employees and trustees are not influenced by the goodies and give something in return to the supplier:

> "[The Department of Labor and the court] took such an outrageously narrow position of what constituted a gratuity," Mr. Braun said.
> "Having the wives of the trustees fly [allegedly to various meetings in Naples, Florida] is not a violation of the law unless it's done as a quid pro quo."[1]

Once a pension fund employee begins accepting the investment manager's schmooze money, it can be a slippery path indeed. Gradually, ever so gradually, people take one small step at a time until they get so far off base it later surprises even them. It is just a matter of time before the line is crossed.

This high-living lifestyle with someone else's checkbook can become addictive, so much so that some pension fund employees might be willing to do almost anything to keep the good times coming. Senior management may even inadvertently speed-up the downhill slide by turning a blind eye toward these "perks." Some senior executives may even take advantage of them themselves.

DISPOSABLE EMPLOYEES

Hardly a week has gone by these past few years without reports of a company laying off thousands of employees. The sad truth is that many of these people got caught up in something that was not of their making and beyond their ability to control. Senior management may have fumbled the ball. They may have made foolish diversification moves that sapped corporate money and attention; they may have designated certain subsidiaries or whole companies as "cash cows" and then milked them without putting money back in to modernize factories and equipment; and they may have allowed bureaucracy to bloat the management ranks and clog the information arteries.

---

1. "Court Upholds Exclusion of Entertainment," *Pension & Investments*, February 7, 1994.

Many senior executives did not see or respond to the changes that were going on around them. Had they exercised just a little foresight, they could have begun making less painful changes, gradually, years ago. Some companies did, but, unfortunately for thousands of employees in other companies, the only alternative became immediate, massive, and painful restructuring.

There was also tremendous peer pressure on senior executives whose companies were not in economic distress to get rid of workers. Management consulting gurus spoke of empowerment. The thought was to restructure, shed employees, and empower the survivors. This would create an environment where the entrepreneurial juices would flow and propel the company to new heights. That may be the ideal, but fear and self-interest is the more likely outcome.

> The implied contract between worker and employer has been broken in an abrupt and harsh way. Whereas a worker's tenure and experience once clearly were assets, now they may be viewed as a liability as firms look to reduce the "head count" and hire young and cheap."[2]

Senior executives never seemed to suffer the same personal economic distress as lower level employees. Indeed, senior managers might have received pay raises for making the "tough decision" to fire someone else, or, if they were eased out, it was with a golden kiss, not a steel-toed boot.

> No matter the quality of their performance, chief executives who are forced to retire often wind up with a bundle. Take W.R. Grace & Co., which awarded recently ousted former chief executive J.P. Bolduc a severance package worth at least $40 million, maybe more. This after allegations of sexual harassment, which finally prompted the board to recommend the Bolduc "should sever his relationship." Bolduc denied the charges but chose not to defend himself before the board.[3]

For many employees, the recent wave of downsizing has been a wake-up call. They are realizing that regardless of how good or how loyal they may have been, the company can and will terminate their employment whenever and however it wants. And senior executives will take care of themselves regardless if they were at the root of the company's problems.

---

2. "No End in Sight to the Unease of U.S. Workers," *Chicago Tribune*, September 25, 1994.
3. "The Cosseted Director," *Forbes*, May 22, 1995.

Faced with this new reality, lower level employees might try to take care of themselves, too. Most employees won't ever cross the line into illegal activities. Others will shun even questionable ones. Some, however, won't care about these distinctions and will use their positions for personal gain whenever they think they can get away with it. "Screw the company because it will screw me" becomes their mantra.

In this type of environment it is also likely that employees will try to hold on to their jobs by doing whatever senior management asks, even if it is questionable, unethical, or, in some instances, even illegal. Do senior executives ask their subordinates to do unethical things? Consider this recent survey of investment analysts. They were first asked whether someone at their company had ever asked them to do something they considered to be unethical.

> Those analysts indicating they had been asked to do something unethical were asked if the request came from a person senior, junior, or at the same level within the organization. For the overwhelming majority of the respondents, *the person was their superior*.[4] [Emphasis added.]

Is fraud in corporations on the rise? Consider what a respected global magazine had to say:

> Fraud is growing exponentially. In 1992, according to a fraud barometer kept by KPMG, an accounting firm, there was a 100% increase [in the U.K. and] . . . it is on course to double again this year to over 1 billion pounds. Ian Huntington of KPMG reckons that increased redundancies among middle managers and reduced corporate loyalty may be partly to blame for the increase in fraud.[5]

And this:

> In a 1993 KPMG Peat Marwick survey of the nation's top companies, 76% of the respondents said they had experienced fraud during the past year. Nearly a fourth of the respondents claimed losses of at least $1 million, and almost two-thirds reported actual or potential losses of more than $100,000.[6]

---

4. "Ethics in the Investment Profession: A Survey," The Research Foundation of The Institute of Chartered Financial Analysts, May 1992.
5. "Serious Fraud Office," *The Economist*, July 10, 1993.
6. "Phar-Mor — A Lesson in Fraud," *The Wall Street Journal*, March 28, 1994.

So the brave new world of the disposable employee has created a harsher corporate environment wherein loyalties and trust may have disintegrated. This provides fertile ground for fraud and wrongdoing to flourish.

CASH KICKBACKS

A broker can make a lot of money trading securities for a pension fund, but first he or she has got to get the business. Most brokers will try by offering a good service at a competitive price. Some will try by schmoozing clients and playing the "old boy" network. Others will go further. They will offer to kickback some of the profit to the person in the pension fund who gave them the account. Here are three examples of the latter. In one company, a pension fund employee allegedly directed trades to a specific broker who in turn kicked back cash and gifts worth $190,000 over the course of several years. These straight cash-for-business arrangements can be very profitable for a broker — this one was reported to have made about $2.5 million as a result of the trades.

Another way to kick back cash involves the way a broker credits an account after a trade has been executed. When an investor places an order to purchase a security at the current price, the broker normally executes the trade as expeditiously as possible and credits the investor's account immediately after the transaction has been completed. In a sophisticated scam, however, the broker executes the trade but does not immediately credit the pension fund's account. Rather, the broker waits to see if subsequent market action makes this trade profitable or not. If it does, the trade is assigned to a special, personal account set up by the pension fund employee, then sold and the profit realized. On the other hand, if subsequent market movements result in a loss, the broker assigns the trade to the pension fund's account. In this way the pension fund's account gets credited with all the losing transactions while the employee's personal account gets credited with all the winning trades and the resulting profits.

A twist on this theme involves the owners of the special account. It does not have to belong to the pension fund employee; it can belong to another individual or entity. Perhaps the account is owned by a friend of the broker or another pension fund that has given the broker a performance-based fee. Better performance, higher fees. For the privilege of being able to direct unprofitable trades to the pension fund's account the broker would have to kick something back to his or her accomplice — the pension fund employee. In one case it was alleged that the broker agreed to kick back 10 percent of the profits in cash and gifts. Over the course of a few years this scam allegedly netted the pension fund employee $315,000. The pension fund, on the other hand, took a hit estimated to be over $3 million in trading losses.

The best place to execute the delay in crediting the account scam is in the mortgage-backed securities sector of the bond market. These securities are mostly traded over-the-counter, which makes pricing less transparent. Moreover, the securities can have settlement dates from a few days to several weeks, so nothing will seem amiss if a trade doesn't settle immediately.

Yet another approach for a chief investment officer looking to collect a little cash is to set up a shell investment management partnership where one of the two partners — in this case the silent partner — is the pension fund employee. All the chief investment officer has to do then is to direct a trade to purchase some securities through this partnership. The partnership executes the trade and collects a commission. In one pension fund the commission was allegedly $25,000 on a $12.5 million trade. If the pension fund lacks internal and external controls and does not have normal due diligence oversight by trustees, the procedure can be easy to execute.

Cold cash payments in exchange for the pension fund's business do not have to come exclusively from rogue brokers. Investment managers and consultants can play the cash kickback game as well. Remember, there are hundreds of thousands of dollars of fees involved, and what's a few dollars slipped under the table? The most straightforward way is for the investment manager or consultant to just pay the chief investment officer some percentage of the fees collected from the pension fund. Yet another way is to inflate the fees so the pension fund pays the kickback. For example, a soft dollar arrangement could be established by the chief investment officer with several brokerage firms. The chief investment officer then instructs several investment managers to buy and sell securities through the designated brokerage firms. Then, a consulting firm submits phony invoices to the brokerage firms for, say, computer services, and receives cash, which is then given to the chief investment officer. No legitimate soft dollar services are provided by the consultant. A similar scam initiated by an investment manager allegedly netted him about $285,000 over the two years the scheme was in operation.

INDIRECT CASH KICKBACKS

Smart chief investment officers avoid receiving cash, at least directly. That is too risky — there isn't a line on the income-tax return for kickbacks, and why give the IRS the chance to pursue them for income-tax evasion and possibly land them in jail? Indirect cash payments are a better way of collecting for the services rendered. If chief investment officers don't take direct cash payments, chances are good the only thing they will lose is their jobs. Such scams can be easily cast as poor judgment.

Consider the potential use of initial public offerings (IPOs). A little background is needed to explain this self-serving strategy. Assume a small, growing company wants to raise capital by selling stock. This is the first time stock in the company is being sold to the public; it is an initial public offering. To accomplish the sale, the company would normally engage the services of an investment banker who would help the company establish the initial offering price and, through an associated brokerage firm, help sell the stock to the public.

There are several different ways to structure the transaction, but that is not relevant here. What is relevant is the determination of the initial offering price. No one really knows for sure what investors will be willing to pay for the stock. Sure, the investment banker might offer some suggestions by comparing what the stock in similar companies sold for in the past and by providing the results of various stock valuation models. But in reality the sales price depends upon what buyers are willing to pay, and no one knows what that will be for sure until the stock starts trading. On one hand, the investment banker would want to see the entire issue sold quickly so that he or she might favor a low offering price. The company, however, would like to get as much money as it can, thus favoring a higher offering price. Even if the company wants a higher price, it still wants to see the entire offering sold. It may need the money for expansion.

Given this uncertainty, there might be times when the initial price is set substantially below what investors are really willing to pay.

The broker gets a feel for this when the initial offering price is published. If lots of investors are banging on the broker's door to buy the
stock chances are good the price will advance sharply when it starts
trading.

How much money could these investors make? One study has
estimated that, on average, an IPO increased 16 percent in the first
day of trading. Remember, though, an investor cannot hope to
achieve those spectacular returns by buying when the stock starts
trading. He or she must buy at the initial offering price *before* the
shares become public. If the investor has been a long-term customer
of the broker and has been generating commissions, his or her
chances of buying at the initial public offering price are better than
those of someone who has not been giving business to the broker:
"Show the broker that you are . . . buttering his bread and as a result
he needs to be nice to you."[7]

This is a perfect arrangement for a chief investment officer who
wants to strong-arm a broker and a broker who wants to return a
favor to a chief investment officer who has been directing millions of
dollars of commissions to his or her firm. The chief investment officer can simply ask the broker for notification of attractive IPOs and
the opportunity to buy the stock at the IPO price. A loan could even
be arranged to finance the transaction. Once the stock goes public,
the chief investment officer would sell his or her shares for a nice
profit. For a $100,000 "investment," on average, the chief investment
officer can expect to make a $16,000 profit in one day. Such "invest-
ments," made several times a year, put the chief investment officer
well on his or her way to leaving the job rich.

If the transaction is kept strictly between the broker and the
chief investment officer, who is to know? Furthermore, if the chief investment officer wants to cement his or her relationship with the boss,
what better way to do so than to inform the boss of a pending IPO?
Some senior executives may never question the chief investment officer as to why the broker is being so solicitous — they would already
know the answer.

Stop and contrast this IPO arrangement with that described in
the earlier section, where the kickback involved direct cash payments.
Both lead to the same end result: cash in the chief investment officer's

---

7. "IPOs: Get in Before Debut or Not at All," *Investor's Business Daily*, June 13, 1994.

pocket. Yet, the IPO approach does not carry the bluntness of a bribe. The chief investment officer can claim that there was no connection between the millions and millions of dollars of trading commissions steered toward the broker and his or her participation in several broker-sponsored IPOs. At worst, senior management might view what transpired with a sense of unease, assuming they even knew about it; at best, they might admire the chief investment officer's investment acumen and ask to be let in on the next IPO.

Lots of money-making tips could come from a brokerage firm. Here is another one. Perhaps a friendly broker might tip off the chief investment officer about some planned junk bond purchases by one of his or her other clients. Since those specific bonds might be in limited supply, a large-scale purchase as planned by the broker's other client could cause the price to rise. If the chief investment officer buys the same security before the other customer, his or her holdings are likely to increase in price when the big order is placed.

Here is another money-making tip. The broker could tip off the chief investment officer just before the brokerage firm changes its earnings forecast or its opinion on a specific stock. Downward changes in estimates or opinions can produce violent price changes. The chief investment officer can place orders beforehand and profit when the bonds or stocks move in the expected direction.

Money-making tips need not be the exclusive domain of the broker. Investment managers can be induced to help, too. For example, say a savings and loan was about to be converted from a mutual company to a stock company, and the investment manager knew this because he or she was a director on the savings and loan's board. To participate, the chief investment officer would have to deposit money in the savings and loan. The deposit qualifies someone to buy the newly offered stock up to the amount of the deposit, dollar for dollar. This is not as attractive a tip as the broker's IPO described above, because it requires the chief investment officer to put up cash, and there is not any strong evidence that the stock would appreciate in price when it started trading.

PERKS OF THE JOB

Pension fund employees, and especially the chief investment officer, are in a position to collect a number of "goodies" from pension fund suppliers. With ever so subtle pressure, suppliers can feel compelled to come through. For example, a chief investment officer can remind the supplier of the pension fund's account size or that the chief investment officer was the one responsible for giving the supplier the pension fund's business. This might be a sufficient hint for the supplier to deliver. The following are some examples of "perks of the job."

A master trustee is typically a subsidiary of a bank. The bank, in turn, offers many services to its customers, one of which is home mortgages. Low interest rates and no points or other closing costs could save a chief investment officer tens of thousands of dollars over the life of the mortgage. The chief investment officer could pressure the pension fund's master trustee contact to arrange a favorable loan with the bank's loan personnel. A similar service could be provided for other senior executives at the company as well.

A more profitable perk, however, is the so-called "tag-along" investment. This involves a pension fund employee investing his or her own money with one of the pension fund's suppliers. When these investments come to light — if they ever do — the standard response from the employee will be that he or she felt so strongly about a particular investment that, in addition to pension fund assets, they wanted to commit some of their own money. No mention need be made of any special arrangements or favorable treatment elicited from the supplier.

Consider real estate. A chief investment officer could approach one of the pension fund's managers to assemble a private venture for the chief investment officer and, perhaps, a few friends, the idea being that they would put up no cash, just a letter of credit, and rely on the investment manager to raise the capital to finance the real estate project. Multimillion-dollar real estate investments might be too much, so they might try something smaller, like an apartment building or a miniwarehouse facility. (Miniwarehouses are self-storage buildings, which individuals and businesses rent on a monthly basis to temporarily store personal belongings or inventories. These facilities are relatively inexpensive to construct, yet could yield high returns.)

How does a chief investment officer make this personal venture a reality? First, he or she has to select and hire an investment manager who specializes in that type of real estate. Then, after allocating pension fund money to the manager, the chief investment officer would raise the issue. Perhaps the real estate manager will bite. If not, maybe even more pension fund money, and the attendant investment manager fees, will do the trick. If auditing procedures are lax and the chief investment officer has been delegated the authority, massive amounts of money might be given to the manager to invest; the investment policy committee being none the wiser. Later, after the chief investment officer leaves, they may discover tens of millions of dollars in transactions they did not approve. By then it's too late.

Another tag-along investment involves the purchase of private stock at attractive prices. Some background is needed to explain this deal. Say an entrepreneur has a great idea for a business but lacks the capital to make it into a reality. The entrepreneur could try to get a bank loan, or ask friends and relatives for money. Another way to raise capital is to sell a portion of the business. The entrepreneur would incorporate and sell some of the shares of stock. But rather than selling the stock to the public as the company would do in an IPO, private investors are sought out. A wide variety of private investors could be available, ranging from wealthy individuals to venture capital firms. Using the power of his or her position, the chief investment officer can inject himself or herself onto the board of directors of the venture capitalist's management firm, the board of directors of the venture capital partnership, or the board of directors of the small, rapidly growing companies in which the venture capital partnership would invest. In fact, it could be made a quid pro quo requirement: If the venture capitalist wants pension fund money, the chief investment officer has to become a director on one of these boards. No directorship, no pension fund money.

In any of these directorship positions, the chief investment officer can then be made aware of private stock, which the chief investment officer can then purchase for his or her own personal account. In addition, if the chief investment officer serves as a director of a small company, part of the remuneration might include stock options. These options could turn into very lucrative investments for the chief investment officer if the small company becomes a high flyer. One investment manager who served as a director on a company in which his mutual fund owned stock received options to purchase 210,000 shares at $3 apiece. With the stock trading on an exchange for $7.50, that amounts to a $945,000 paper profit.

The chief investment officer is also in a position to help the company expand. For example, should the small company need additional capital, a direct loan from the pension fund might be arranged, or pressure could be put on one of the pension fund's venture capitalists to come up with the loan. Should the small company want to go public, the chief investment officer could help arrange the services of an investment banker. When the company goes public the chief investment officer could encourage the pension fund's investment managers to buy the stock.

Using one's position to promote an investment that an individual already owns happens in the industry. Consider a consultant who fails to adequately disclose that his firm, and the consultant himself, has a financial interest in a venture capital partnership that he was recommending to a pension fund investment committee. Or consider a financial advisor who steered trustees into high-risk investments on which he collected large commissions, and encouraged them to invest in companies in which he is a partial owner. Or consider brokerage firm personnel who tout an investment in certain real estate securities their firm owns, but then do not adequately reveal the true financial condition of the firm on which the investment's success depends. If pension fund suppliers can use their positions to promote an investment in which they have a personal stake, it is naive to think a chief investment officer cannot do the same.

The opportunity for money making perks is incredible. The chief investment officer, however, could also be at the receiving end of some pretty nice entertainment provided by pension fund suppliers. This perk warrants an entire section of its own.

ENTERTAINMENT

There is nothing inherently wrong with business entertainment. Breakfasts, lunches, an occasional dinner, or tickets to a ballgame are all part of the way business is conducted. The twist that makes it questionable is when the entertainment is requested by the chief investment officer and/or when it goes way beyond what is normally considered reasonable. Entertainment then becomes a way of repaying the chief investment officer for the privilege of doing business with the pension fund.

Some examples of things that might be considered over the line are extravagant parties, tickets plus airfare to the World Series and Super Bowl, Cuban cigars, Hermés ties, special gifts to friends, and frequent dinners with spouses at the top restaurants. Free tickets for any theater performance, sporting event, or concert are there for the asking. Sometimes, in order to impress, the entertainment needs to be very lavish indeed. Tastes improve with surprising speed. The players involved can be consultants, investment managers, and brokers.

The chief investment officer can also induce his or her subordinates into playing by requesting them to alter expense vouchers. For example, say the boss wants to take some subordinates, friends, and their spouses out to dinner. No problem; the chief investment officer can just tell one of the subordinates to pick up the tab and voucher it off to the pension fund. Since the boss approves the voucher, no one at the company will be any the wiser. And the goodies don't have to stop with food — the boss can request personal items as well.

Some of the chief investment officer's subordinates might get fed up with this chicanery but be fearful of retaliation if they say anything. They might just pay the bill out of their own pockets and count it as a cost of working for this chief investment officer. Others might dive in and enjoy the perks themselves.

Some pension fund suppliers will take it upon themselves to supply little "goodies" to pension fund employees. For example, one employee was planning a trip to Toronto to help a consulting firm construct an asset allocation model for exclusive use by his pension fund. The employee declined an invitation by the manager to dinner, saying his wife was going to accompany him and they would be visiting relatives that night. When the manager sent over the meeting agenda there, in the packet, was an airline ticket for his wife paid for by the consultant.

When it comes to lavish parties, however, the chief investment officer can't be too blatant. If these parties were only for the chief investment officer and his or her guests, it might raise eyebrows. One way around this is to allow the firms that are paying the bill to invite other clients. Not too many, however; just enough so that to an outsider it appears as if the party was really business entertainment initiated by the paying firms rather than by the chief investment officer.

A chief investment officer might even set up a slush fund to take care of some miscellaneous expenses. One way to do this is to create a special project for a consultant with the tacit understanding that the consultant's fee is to be used to pay for the chief investment officer's "requests." It is often easier to get higher management to pay a consultant's bill than to ask for reimbursement for these expenditures. If a subordinate raises the issue with the chief investment officer's boss, he or she can claim the extras are just the way the consultant entertains clients. The connection between the "goodies" and the make-work project is blurred.

The chief investment officer can become a Santa Claus, using the pension fund suppliers to provide gifts to anyone he or she chooses. If the chief investment officer wants to have dinner with the boss and his wife in a high-class restaurant, no problem. The chief investment officer can invite an investment manager along and instruct the manager to pick up the tab. A chief investment officer can provide expensive retirement gifts by first asking subordinates for donations, then asking an investment manager to silently kick in the rest. On the surface, it looks like the employees were very generous. Bottles of champagne can be sent to a honeymooning friend by just telling a consultant when and where to deliver the champagne. It is like having an unlimited credit card, with someone else paying the bills.

Eventually this might all come back to the pension fund in the form of higher expenses, so a little creativity is needed. First, the chief investment officer must make sure the bills are paid out of the pension fund, not the corporate budget. Out of sight, out of mind. Second, some of the expenses need to be reclassified so that expenses don't look out of line. The easiest ones to reclassify are real estate investment management fees. Technically they should be classified the same way as other management fees. However, if part of the fee includes services to acquire a property, a chief investment officer might argue that it should be classified as a "capital" expenditure and added to the property's purchase price. Presto, the investment management fee disappears. Anyone, including senior executives, who were evaluating the pension fund's expenses as they related to the size of assets might erroneously conclude expenses were low. Reclassification of expenses would allow the chief investment officer the opportunity to increase the reported expenses yet still seem within guidelines for other pension funds.

Reclassifying expenses is one way to make reported expenses appear lower than they really are. Another approach is to change the investment strategy for one or more investment types to actually lower expenses in those areas in order to give the chief investment officer more room to increase expenses in another. For example, passive management has lower investment management fees, so if a chief investment officer introduces this style into the investment strategy he or she can then increase expenses in another area without affecting the total. Chances are good that senior management will never analyze the fees paid item by item.

Second, a lot of those goodies can be recouped by a brokerage firm in the bid/ask spread. Chances are good here, too, that senior management will not get into the details. If they do ask about trading costs, a friendly consultant could always justify them as being reasonable. Again, no one need be the wiser.

Finally, directed brokerage can be used to pay many consulting bills. Senior executives may not even be aware of this way to compensate pension fund suppliers.

Increased expenses, however, is not the greatest damage that can be done to a pension fund by this activity. A chief investment officer might be more lenient at performance review time with a pension fund supplier who was generous with the goodies. Poorly performing investment managers who should have been fired years ago might be kept on; sloppy consulting reports might be accepted; and detailed analyses of trading costs might be neglected. The true impact on plan participants could be in the millions of dollars.

JOBS

A chief investment officer is in the position to be a source of jobs. For example, say the spouse of the company's senior auditor is looking for employment. The chief investment officer could encourage a consultant to hire the spouse to work on the pension fund's account. A chief investment officer also could help arrange a job for the boss when he retires. Or, a trustee job could be arranged for a senior executive of the company with a mutual fund sponsored by a brokerage firm that does millions of dollars of trades for the pension fund. But why stop there? The chief investment officer could be instrumental in hiring the firm of one of the members of the board of directors, or even setting up one of his or her own friends in business as a pension fund supplier. The opportunities are seemingly limitless.

Some would argue that there is nothing wrong here and this type of thing happens all the time in business. People network with suppliers and get jobs for others; this is just an example of human nature that could occur anywhere in a company, not just in pension fund administration.

Sure, the auditor, the boss, and the senior executive might not let the chief investment officer's largess influence their diligence or their fiduciary responsibilities. Then again, they might be more willing to appreciate the chief investment officer's view on pension fund ethics when establishing a pension fund code of conduct, or be more lenient at appraisal time, or even cut the chief investment officer some slack when evaluating specific investment alternatives. That is the downside when a chief investment officer acts as an employment agency for company executives.

NEST FEATHERING

The opportunities for a chief investment officer to use his or her position as a stepping stone to bigger and better things are also seemingly limitless. The most straightforward way is for a chief investment officer to allocate a substantial sum of pension fund money to an investment manager and then leave the pension fund to join that manager's firm.

Another, more sophisticated way is to use a pension fund supplier to create a new company in which the chief investment officer would have an ownership stake. Say a major bank wants to sell its investment management unit. While the chief investment officer would like to make the acquisition as a personal venture, it might require far too much money to raise individually. However, if the chief investment officer interests one of the pension fund's investment managers, perhaps the investment manager will make the acquisition and, with proper "hints" along the way by the chief investment officer, turn to him or her to head-up the new firm. It's a gutsy move, but the chief investment officer has little to lose. The pension fund might have a real estate manager, for example, who is thinking about diversifying its business into stock and bond money management. When a bank puts its investment management business on the block, a chief investment officer might jump at the opportunity to put a deal together with the real estate manager as the buyer. The chief investment officer could even use the resources of the pension fund to help the deal along. First, a substantial amount of pension fund assets could be allocated to the real estate investment manager to create a few IOUs.

Next, pension fund resources could be used to evaluate the acquisition, to develop a business plan, and to assess what price should be offered for the investment management unit. Finally, other pension fund suppliers might be approached to become minority investors in the new operation.

Another way to lay the groundwork for a later move while picking up some extra income now is for a chief investment officer to set himself or herself up as a part-time investment manager catering to high-net-worth individuals. If the fledging firm takes off, he or she can jump to it full time. But there are two major problems: (1) having products to sell, and (2) getting the high-net-worth clients.

One product is investment advice. A chief investment officer has access to a lot of investment information. This could be a highly salable product. Another product is mutual funds. Sale commissions, or finder fees, are sometimes paid by mutual funds for new business. A chief investment officer might be able to "persuade" one of the pension fund's investment managers to give the chief investment officer a finder's fee on any assets that he or she can steer to the investment manager's mutual funds.

Now, consider how to go about getting clients. Some of these might just come naturally; perhaps the chief investment officer's colleagues, and even senior executives, might be asking him or her for investment advice. It would be fairly easy to steer these individuals into the investment manager's mutual funds and collect the finder's fee.

Another way for the chief investment officer to get clients is to hire a salesperson to beat the bushes. The salesperson could work full-time in a small firm established by the chief investment officer. The chief investment officer could then stay with the pension fund and supply investment advice to the small firm's clients.

Yet another way to gain entry into the high-net-worth marketplace is to use the pension fund's assets. The two most promising sources of high-net-worth individuals accessible to the chief investment officer are those in venture capital and real estate. Consider venture capital investments. If the chief investment officer allocates a lot of the pension fund's money to these partnerships and becomes a board member on several of them, perhaps he or she can do some effective networking with other investors, many of whom are high-net-worth individuals who might be in need of the chief investment officer's services.

Real estate is another area the chief investment officer might use to network with high-net-worth individuals and prospective clients. A particularly good approach is to do a deal with a well-known celebrity who might not be familiar with investments and who can provide access to other high-net-worth individuals.

HIRING A FRIENDLY PENSION FUND SUPPLIER

What makes a number of these schemes work is the ability to steer a friendly supplier into the pension fund's stable. For a clever chief investment officer that's not too hard.

A chief investment officer could just go out and hire a friendly consultant, but a better approach is to conduct a review of several as a cover. An even better approach is to let staff conduct the analysis so as to give the appearance of impartiality on the part of the chief investment officer. For example, say the chief investment officer asks his or her staff to evaluate prospective candidates for the job. A list of four names comes up, including a candidate "suggested" by the chief investment officer. Staff takes the job seriously and conducts a series of in-depth interviews. After the interviews, and according to a pre-established list of criteria, staff ranks the candidates as they saw them. The chief investment officer's suggested candidate ranks dead last. What can the chief investment officer do? Just change the selection criteria. Presto, the "desired" candidate moves up in rank to first. If anyone asks, a study was done and this consultant came out on top according to this set of criteria. The chief investment officer would not stop there, however. The next likely step would be to rearrange staff responsibilities so that people who conduct future studies are more in tune with the chief investment officer's "philosophy."

Once a friendly consultant is on board, he or she can be used to hire a friendly investment manager. A chief investment officer, for example, could present a case to fire one of the existing managers. This would create an open spot. Or, the chief investment officer could simply decide to increase the number of investment managers on the pension fund's team, informing senior management that the increase in the size of the pension fund requires more managers. The bigger the pension fund grows, the more managers it needs. No mention need be made of alternate ways of dealing with that growth in assets.

Another way is to focus on the positive aspects of a particular manager and completely ignore the investment strategy developed for that investment type. Yet another is to change the investment strategy such that it calls for the hiring of more managers.

Once a decision to hire a new manager has been made, the next step is to manipulate the selection process. The chief investment officer could start by asking the friendly consultant to prepare a list of prospective investment managers. When discussing the project, the chief investment officer would just happen to mention the name of the "favored" investment manager. With a few additional comments, such as how much the chief investment officer *really* likes this specific manager, the consultant (unlike staff in the earlier example) will get the message. The consultant can just rationalize that the final selection is not up to him or her and go ahead and add the "favored" candidate's name to the list.

A list of finalists, including the candidate the chief investment officer wants to hire, would then be developed. At this point (in some pension funds) the list would go to the investment policy committee for final selection. With any degree of skill, the chief investment officer can easily tilt the presentation toward the desired investment manager. It doesn't take much, just a few negative comments about the other finalists. Also, a smart chief investment officer would recommend that only a small amount of pension fund assets be given to this new manager as a test. The committee will like that approach. In other pension funds the chief investment officer would make the selection, the consultant's study being no more than a cover in case anyone later questioned the decision.

Make no mistake: If the chief investment officer controls the flow of information, and has the help of a friendly consultant, the chief investment officer will control the decision. Once hired, it is very easy to increase the amount of pension assets that manager has to manage. Within a few years, the friendly manager could become the largest investment manager for the pension fund and be collecting millions of dollars in management fees.

The chief investment officer can also use the agenda of the investment policy committee meetings to his or her advantage. For example, one approach a chief investment officer might use to get venture capital firms hired is to place the request for their approval at the end of a long investment policy committee meeting where, earlier, multimillion-dollar asset allocation decisions are discussed. Since venture capital investments are typically made in smaller, $2 to $5 million increments, a large pension fund might consider these commitments as trivial. In this way, the chief investment officer could get every recommended venture capital firm approved.

Getting real estate deals approved is a bit trickier because of their size and because attorneys and appraisers might be involved, but it can be done. Consider this: Say the real estate investment involved a high-net-worth individual, and the chief investment officer very much wants to do this deal. However, from an investment viewpoint it is not particularly attractive. There is excess property of this type on the market already, the economy is softening in this area, the team that will oversee the development lacks experience, and the deal has had little interest from other investors. Still, the chief investment officer wants to proceed. If that's the case, the presentation to the internal committee could be packaged in the most favorable light. No one on the committee need know that an extraordinary set of very favorable events would have to occur for the property to achieve anywhere near the returns projected by the chief investment officer. For example, it could be argued that the deal would offer a 20 percent annual return with minimal downside risk because the venture's inherent land value would protect the pension fund's principle investment. That's a pretty good return with minimal risk. Some committees will not even think of asking that return projections on a real estate project be calculated under a worst-case scenario; will not even bother to visit the property before it is approved for acquisition; and, if they request an independent appraisal, will let the chief investment officer select the appraiser.

However, even with attractive numbers a chief investment officer might not want to risk a committee meeting. To avoid that, a "divide and conquer" strategy can be used. This involves the chief investment officer first planting a seed that a real estate joint venture is being seriously considered. This could be done at a regular investment policy committee meeting. The chief investment officer might even be able to leave the impression that he or she is negotiating hard to cut the best deal and that when the chief investment officer seeks approval, the committee has to act fast or the deal will collapse.

The next step is for the chief investment officer to convince one of the committee members to approve the investment. The best member might be the chief investment officer's boss. Once that's done, the chief investment officer and that committee member would go to the highest ranking person on the committee. With two people pitching the project, and a reminder the pension fund has to act fast or the deal will be taken by someone else, the highest ranking committee member is likely to okay the investment. Group dynamics suggest that it is difficult for one individual to withstand a majority opinion, especially when the issue is surrounded with unknowns and "expert" opinions. Once the senior ranking committee member has given the okay, the other committee members will fall into line. Psychologically, it would be very difficult for them to request a full meeting after the most senior person has signed on. Presto, the investment has been approved without a full meeting of the investment policy committee.

Choosing with one's self in mind is a universal experience; it's human nature. We have all made decisions between two alternatives simply because we liked one more than the other. That's *not* what has been outlined in this section — these are examples of a chief investment officer *intentionally* biasing a decision to hire a pension fund supplier to achieve some sort of personal gain. This is wrong, yet, as you can see, is so very easy to pull off and so very easy to hide.

CHURNING

This term is used to describe a rogue broker rapidly trading securities in an individual's account in order to generate commissions. The more trades the broker executes, the more commission income he or she can generate.

The same idea can be applied to an entire pension fund, but on a much grander scale, initiated not by the broker but by the chief investment officer. It would involve initiating the trading of huge quantities of pension fund securities and then directing as much of the trading activity as possible to the favored broker. The broker would reap millions in trading revenue and, in turn, do something "nice" for the chief investment officer — a bit of mutual backscratching.

There are three areas where a chief investment officer can initiate trading activity: shifts between investment types, changes in investment strategy, and/or hiring or firing investment managers. First consider shifts between investment types or asset mix changes. At any point in time there are investment advisors who think the stock market is about to go up and others who think it is about to go down. Both buyers and sellers will have lots of good reasons to justify their opinions. That is the nature of investment markets. All a chief investment officer has to do is to selectively gather the "facts" to "prove" whichever side he or she wants to take — market up or market down — then present these selected facts to the investment committee and get its approval to proceed. Once the committee has approved the change in the asset mix, the chief investment officer might be given free rein to execute the decision, including selecting a broker to execute the trades. The chief investment officer could then channel the transaction to a friendly broker. Later, he or she can simply say market conditions have changed and recommend another asset mix change, generating even more commissions.

It is possible that a chief investment officer can completely bypass the committee and execute a trade without its approval or knowledge. To initiate such a trade — say a sale of international bonds and a purchase of international stocks — requires that the chief investment officer already have in place an investment manager who manages multiple investment types. That manager would have been given the authority to execute trades on behalf of the pension fund without prior approval.

Step one is for the chief investment officer to convince the investment manager to sell the pension fund's international bonds and to use the proceeds to buy international stocks. This task should not be too difficult if the investment manager's fee is large. The unsubtle threat that the chief investment officer will remove the assets and place them with another manager generally will be enough to seal the trading decision. Step two is for the chief investment officer to get the investment manager to use the favored broker to execute the trades. This is trickier. The chief investment officer can give instructions, but the investment manager's staff might not listen. If that happens, the chief investment officer can always make life rough for the investment manager and his or her staff. Another "solution" is for the chief investment officer to instruct one of his or her own staff members to oversee the transaction and make sure the investment manager's staff uses the "right" broker. However, assume this pension fund staff member is conscientious, really looking out for the pension fund's interest. So as not to offend the chief investment officer, but still get the best deal for the pension fund, a quasi-competitive bidding program might be arranged without the chief investment officer's or the favored broker's knowledge. This simply involves getting quotes from other brokers before asking for the favored broker's bid. Armed with these competitive quotes, the favored broker could beat or meet the prices of the other brokers and get the business. If not, one of the other brokers would get the business.

If discovered, the chief investment officer would not be very happy with this arrangement, either. The reason the chief investment officer wanted the staff member to supervise the transaction was to get the favored broker all the business. If a staff member was to act this independently, the chief investment officer might decide to rearrange staff responsibilities. The point is simply this: A determined chief investment officer will eventually get his or her way even if it means a complete turnover of investment managers or pension fund personnel.

It is entirely possible that the decision to make a shift in assets from one investment type to another is in the best interests of plan participants. However, the execution of this strategy allows a self-serving chief investment officer to reap personal benefits. Thus, that "appropriate" decision to shift assets might cost plan participants millions of dollars in unnecessarily high trading costs. Senior executives might not even ask who executes the trades, how much they cost, or what were the alternatives. Too many "details." Even though this is a fiduciary's responsibility, it could be simply too much detail for some committees.

CHAPTER 8

The Threat of Inside Abuse

While much abuse can be visited on a pension fund from willing suppliers and a compliant chief investment officer, the chief investment officer and his or her bosses can also extract personal benefits from the pension fund's assets on their own. This chapter outlines some of the "perks" that can be taken by senior executives.

PLAN TERMINATIONS

One reason a company would want to terminate its pension plan is because it believes it has no other choice. It feels the pension costs are so burdensome it has become a life-or-death situation — jettison the pension promise or bury the company. General mismanagement of the company, resulting in financial distress and bankruptcy, is the most frequent cause of insider abuse.

A healthy company, however, might want to terminate its pension plan to recapture the so-called "excess" pension fund assets. This can occur either by the company's own management taking action or as a result of a merger or acquisition. The process could go something like this. First, the board of directors would vote to terminate the pension plan. Next, the company's actuaries would determine the size of the pension promise. Then the PBGC would review and sign off on the termination. Next, the company's senior executives would seek an insurance company that would be willing to take over the company's retirement promises. The transfer of the company's pension promise to the insurance company would be effected through the purchase of annuity contracts sold by the insurance company. The money used to buy these contracts would come from the pension fund. Any money remaining in the fund (less applicable taxes) would then be transferred into the company's checking account.

Once the money is out of the pension fund and in the company's checking account, senior executives can do whatever they like with it: pay back the money they borrowed to acquire the company; buy back some of the company's stock to increase senior management's ownership position; acquire new factories and equipment; build a new headquarters; or buy a new corporate jet. There are many ways senior executives can spend this pension fund "windfall."

If an insurance company now has responsibility for the pension promise, why should plan participants care? Consider the example of the company that terminated its pension plan and transferred the pension promise to the Executive Life Insurance Company, which subsequently went bankrupt. Being bankrupt, the insurance company couldn't make good on the payments. Moreover, since the pension plan was terminated, under current rules, the PBGC safety net no longer applied. Here are scenes from the resulting nightmare:

> Along with 84,000 other Executive Life annuity holders in 46 states, Lillian Finan, 69 and now living month to month, worries whether she will lose her only steady income. "What am I going to do?" she wonders. "Is somebody going to give me a job? And why should I have to do that after my husband and I worked so hard for all of those years?"[1]
>
> "The little man's going to lose, it doesn't make any difference which way you turn." Clarence Lawson rolls the words over carefully in his mouth. "I believed from day one that the pension money could never be moved. We just got stuck." Lawson, 65, is one of almost 13,000 past and present Fieldcrest-Cannon textile workers who put their trust in the boss and lost out.[2]
>
> Perelman shut down Revlon's pension plan and skimmed off at least $50 million in "excess funding." He then rolled existing pension obligations into Executive Life annuities. Says Eli Schefer, a retired

---

1. "Is Your Pension Safe?," *Time*, June 3, 1991.
2. "Poached Nest Eggs — Out in the Cold at Cannon Mills," *The Nation*, September 16, 1991.

Revlon engineer in Sands Point, N.Y.: "Those were cozy deals, not done according to fiduciary standards. These guys should be thrown in jail. Now that I am almost 72, I've got to worry about when my next pension check is coming, and from where it is coming. It's outrageous."[3]

Did senior executives skim assets? Were they insufficiently conservative? Was there a breach of fiduciary responsibilities? Was choosing Executive Life an act of fraud, coziness, poor analysis, or just bad luck?

Certainly a company, its actuaries, the insurance company, and others who were involved in making the decisions will put their own spin on events, and the buck will be passed. The company will say "Gosh, we terminated the plan and transferred our responsibilities to the insurance company. We have no further obligations. If you have a problem, go see the insurance company." The insurance company will say "Gosh, we made some poor investment decisions and we're sorry, but we're bankrupt. We can't pay. Go see the PBGC." The PBGC will say "Gosh, we're sorry too, but the company terminated the plan and the obligations were transferred to the insurance company. Our safety net applies only to covered plans and yours is no longer covered. In fact, you no longer have a plan; it has been terminated. We can't be expected to pick up any of the obligations for plans that no longer fall under our jurisdiction. Sorry."

Pretty scary, isn't it? Unless some laws are changed, it seems that everyone, except the plan participant, is off the hook. Sure, they could file a lawsuit, but against whom and on what grounds? Sure, some state insurance agency might help, but to what extent? Then there are the legal fees, delays, and hassles. Plan participants could be pushed into this quagmire just because some senior executives decided it was in *their* best interests to terminate the pension plan and they pressured board members, including the trustees of the pension plan, into taking the appropriate steps to terminate the pension plan. They might take the view that these are the company's assets and the company's senior executives will decide what to do with them.

Several years ago, the government was moved to increase the tax on the "excess" assets recovered from the pension fund as a result of a plan termination. That has seemed to make plan terminations less

3. "Is Your Pension Safe?," *Time*, June 3, 1991.

appealing to companies. Remember, though, that companies still retain the right to terminate their pension plan, and plan participants may not have a say in the decision or in the process. In addition, the wreckage of Executive Life is still working its way through the courts, so the ground rules are in the process of being changed. Moreover, various laws have also been proposed in Congress. These have been subjected to intense behind-the-scenes industry lobbying efforts.

Many emotions come into play when a company becomes the target of a takeover or merger. On one hand, senior executives might be reluctant to relinquish the reins of power. They may have nurtured the company along, and it has become the love of their lives. On the other hand, they know they could become extremely wealthy individuals:

> Kemper Corp., battling an unfriendly $2.2 billion takeover offer from GE Capital Corp., has set up a lucrative compensation plan for its top 13 executives if they leave as a result of a change of control, according to Kemper's proxy statement . . . Under the compensation plan, the top five executives could receive at least an estimated $19.4 million if the company is sold.[4]

Kemper isn't alone. Many large companies have these so-called "golden parachutes" to protect their senior executives.

Board members who are charged with the responsibility for making the decisions are also faced with conflicts. They need to consider the interests of shareowners who may be offered a substantial premium over the current market price for the company's stock. Yet, what is being offered in a takeover might be considered inadequate. Board members also might feel allegiance to the existing senior management team, and some board members are trustees of the company's pension fund. The fact is, there can be many cross-currents of corporate and self-interest in the ranks of senior executives and board members when a company becomes the target of a takeover or merger.

However, the target company's pension fund can be a pawn in these high-level maneuvers. It could be put out of reach of unwanted suitors by the company not because of some altruism on the part of senior executives, but rather because of their desire to control the

---

4. "Kemper Plans Lucrative Compensation for Top Executives If Firm Is Acquired," *The Wall Street Journal*, March 29, 1994.

process. They do this by making sure the pension plan document has a provision stating that any excess assets in the pension fund (one of the things a corporate raider might want to get his or her hands on) becomes the property of plan participants. Consider this paragraph from one company's plan document:

> In the event that a Change in Control . . . occurs and the Plan is terminated . . . no Plan assets shall directly or indirectly revert to the Company . . . and any Excess Assets . . . shall be used exclusively to provide retirement benefits . . . [Note: Change in control was defined as someone suddenly buying more than 20 percent of the company's stock or making a tender offer to buy the entire company.]

This company went even further and put in its plan provisions to block the combining of its pension plan with that of the unwanted suitor. One technique raiders used was to combine their underfunded plan with the target company's well-funded plan and then at some later date terminate the new, combined plan.

However, all these comforting antitakeover provisions can be changed by the company's board of directors, and the path to the pension fund's assets can be cleared. The antitakeover provisions are simply barriers which senior executives can remove if it is in their best interests to do so. And therein lies the rub. While senior executives collect on their golden parachutes, plan participants — and the pension promise — can be adversely impacted, and plan participants have no say in the process:

> [Karen Ferguson of the Pension Rights Center] described what happened to a 51-year-old who had worked for a company almost 30 years and would have soon been eligible for its generous early-retirement program. When his company was acquired, his job did not change, but his early-retirement benefit dropped from $22,000 if he retired at age 55 to just $12,000 a year. The possibility of the rules changing at the end of the road has shocked some workers.[5]

Benefits already earned should stay intact, but any that have yet to be earned, including special early retirement benefits, can be changed by the new board of directors. Moreover, the new board can terminate the pension plan of the acquired company, combine it with another plan, or change expectations for any further increases.

---

5. "How Safe Is Your Pension?" *Pittsburgh Post-Gazette*, July 11, 1994.

Millions of dollars in golden parachutes can be made in a merger or acquisition even though the company's cash-rich pension fund suffers in the process.

USING THE PENSION FUND
TO INCREASE EXECUTIVE PAY

Many companies offer their most senior executives earnings-driven compensation packages. These come in many forms such as stock options, stock grants, and, more recently, setting benchmarks for corporate earnings growth and other financial targets which, if achieved, can result in huge cash bonuses. For example, one corporation offered seven of its most senior executives the opportunity to earn up to $4.5 million a year each if certain financial objectives were achieved. This, in addition to tens of thousands of shares in stock options and grants, can make senior executives extremely wealthy.

> Many chief executives find their jobs an enriching experience these days, thanks to boards' intensified pursuit of outside talent, swollen profit, a takeover boom and the lessened uproar about executive pay. "Greed clearly is back in style," says Robert Monks, a principal of Lens, Inc., an activist investment fund in Washington. "There is almost a feeling [among CEOs] that the money is there to be taken."[6]

In many cases, over half of a senior executive's compensation can be performance-based and related in some way to increasing corporate earnings. This is good news for many senior executives; given the leverage offered by these performance incentives they have the opportunity to make a fortune. It is also good news for shareowners — under these incentive schemes, shareowners can be reasonably confident that a senior executive's self-interest will be aligned with theirs. Both would like to see the price of the company's stock increase.

It may not be such great news for pension plan participants, however. Corporate contributions to the pension fund are an expense, and senior executives who are financially motivated to increase corporate earnings will be looking for ways to cut expenses.

But surely senior executives who are also participants in the company's pension plan wouldn't do anything to jeopardize their own pension benefits, would they? Perhaps not. But consider this. Some

6. "Raking It In," *The Wall Street Journal*, April 12, 1995.

senior executives have a proportionally less personal stake in the financial well-being of the pension fund than other employees. Most of these senior executives' financial security comes from the wealth they have accumulated along the way and from other retirement plans the company has set up for them. If they can increase corporate earnings, they can increase their wealth more than any payment from the pension fund would offer them.

Here is an example. Say a chief executive officer has a fixed salary of $1.4 million a year, plus the potential for another $1.4 million if certain earnings targets are achieved. Also, say the executive has been given options on thousands of shares of the company's stock and is entitled to a $750,000 yearly pension. Because of government imposed Section 415 limitations (as discussed in Chapter 3), perhaps only $100,000 of the promised $750,000 retirement income can legally be paid out of the company's pension fund. The remaining $650,000 comes from a special supplemental plan, set up by the company specifically to make up for this shortfall. So the senior executive could be faced with a choice of either increasing the company's contributions to the pension fund, which would help secure his or her future $100,000 yearly retirement income, or reducing the company's contributions, which would increase corporate earnings and thus help secure his or her $1.4 million performance bonus.

This does not even take into consideration the millions of dollars in increased wealth should higher corporate earnings cause a jump in the price of the company's stock. For example, one chief executive officer signed on with a company in April of 1994. In addition to his $1 million yearly salary he was awarded options to purchase 750,000 shares of his company's stock at $38 each. After taking "restructuring" steps, the stock's price increased to $77 a share less than a year later, making his options worth a whopping $29 million.

Adding impetus to this move toward performance-based compensation for senior executives is the government. Section 162(m) of the 1993 tax reform bill caps the tax deductibility of the salaries of the most senior executives at publicly traded companies at $1 million per year. If a company wants to pay more, it must either forego the tax deduction of the additional amount or offer a qualifying performance-based plan.

Paying for performance makes sense at all levels of a company. If an employee contributes to the general welfare of the company, he or she should be compensated accordingly. That's not an issue. The issue is whether in striving for increased corporate earnings in order to achieve greater compensation, pension plan participants are short-changed. The likelihood of this happening increases when there is no one in the boardroom who is looking out for the interests of pension plan participants.

Many senior executives do a good job of balancing the pension plan participant's long-term need for a sound pension fund with their own need to increase short-term corporate earnings. Others live and die by short-term results. They want earnings — and their compensation — to increase, and now.

Pension plans, as well as retiree health care benefits, are big-ticket expense items. These areas will attract the attention of senior executives who are looking for ways to reduce expenses. Moreover, these lucrative, performance-based compensation packages give some senior executives strong motivation to take action because it will be in their own personal interests to do so.

Faced with a choice between increasing the security of the pension promise or increasing corporate earnings and, thus, one's own wealth, some executives will opt for the latter. The reality of it is that retirees are out of sight, out of mind. They are often thought of only in terms of a "liability." If push came to shove in many of the boardrooms in America and the choice was between increased earnings or increased retiree security, which do you think a board would choose?

There are plenty of pension fund levers senior executives can pull to improve corporate earnings. They can fiddle with the plan's assumptions. Consider the mortality rate used to calculate the company's pension liability. We all know we're going to die; the question is when. If a company assumes a retiree will die 10 years after retirement, then 10 years' worth of retirement checks are necessary. On the other hand, if they assume five years, then only five years' worth of retirement checks are needed. The faster plan participants are assumed to die, the lower will be the plan's liabilities. The lower the liabilities, the less money needed in the pension fund and the less the company needs to contribute. The less a company contributes, the higher its corporate earnings. Presto, an "aggressive" mortality assumption leads to higher corporate earnings than they would have been, all else being equal.

They can also fiddle with the investment rate. As described in Chapter 4, this is the rate used to estimate the present value of future pension promises. The higher the assumed investment rate, the lower the plan's liabilities. Over the past 10 years or so, stock and bond market returns have been outstanding. These investments had a wonderful run, and pension funds (as well as other investors) who were lucky enough to catch it made lots of money. This increase in the pension fund's investment returns allowed companies to stop their contributions. Today, however, the investment outlook for the future might not be as spectacular as it was in the past, so a lower value might be prudent. Yet, senior executives might be reluctant to lower their assumptions to more realistic levels because that might have a negative impact on corporate earnings:

> A Kidder Peabody & Co. study attributed 44% of the gain in corporate earnings between 1982 and 1987 to a decline in pension expense. But now that returns in the capital market have fallen, companies are reluctant to give back the gains . . .[7]

Indeed:

> Lowering interest rate assumptions by two percentage points would result in a 21% hit to [a company's] per share earnings . . .[8]

Is a company doing anything wrong by using a higher investment assumption or a faster death rate or are they just engaging in wishful thinking? Without being privy to the discussions when the decision was made, we really don't know for sure. The rub is that these decisions are made behind closed doors by those whose salaries are tied to increases in corporate earnings. If they are using "aggressive" assumptions a pension fund might be seriously underfunded, yet, from the outside looking in, everything seems okay.

Second, senior executives might use the pension fund to increase corporate earnings by transferring pension fund assets and plan liabilities. Consider transferring assets. A pension-law provision, passed by Congress, allows companies to use the excess assets in the pension fund to pay retiree medical expenses. One company reported in its 1994 annual report:

7. "Retirees at Risk," *The Wall Street Journal*, September 2, 1993.
8. "The Pain of Assumptions," *Pension & Investment*, May 2, 1994.

During 1993 the company utilized approximately $90 million in excess pension assets to help pay the nonmanagement retiree health care obligations.

Typically these health care costs are paid out of the company's checkbook and have an impact on corporate earnings, either directly or as contributions to a company sponsored health care trust fund. However, if money is transferred out of the pension fund to help pay health care costs, any negative impact on corporate earnings might be eliminated. It's like robbing Peter (the pension fund) to pay Paul (the health care commitment) to avoid any negative impact on corporate earnings.

Next, consider transferring liabilities. This involves shifting some of the company's underfunded liabilities in an hourly pension plan to a well-funded salary plan. In the past, these transfers were hit with a tax that, for all practical purposes, stopped them from occurring. But a recent IRS ruling which approved the transfer between two plans — one underfunded and the other well-funded — might signal the way for more pension funds to follow suit:

> The private letter ruling — given to an unknown company — could help scores of companies reduce their pension liabilities without putting extra money or paying a penalty.[9]

Third, some companies may entice their employees to give up current salary increases in exchange for better future retirement benefits. Trading off salary increases now for future retirement benefits may sound like a good deal at the time, and it may be. Sadly, however, it is possible some senior executives may have entered into that promise never intending to keep it. It is easy to make promises and just let some future management team or government agency worry about the implications. Consider this:

> Money losing corporations sometimes promise their employees generous benefits in lieu of wage hikes or simply scrimp on pension contributions figuring at worst that other employers — via the PBGC — ultimately will have to pick up the tab.[10]

---

9. "Sponsors May Shift Some Underfunded Liability," *Pension and Investments*, June 14, 1993.

10. "The Crying Game Over Pensions," *Business Week*, April 5, 1993.

Promises in exchange for lower wages mean better short-term corporate earnings, all else being equal. If senior executives have pulled a fast one and pension fund contributions have not increased to pay for these promises, the true impact of what has happened won't be felt until years into the future. By that time, current management will be long gone, leaving another senior management team (and possibly the PBGC) to worry about picking up the pieces.

Finally, senior executives might use the pension fund to increase corporate earnings by increasing the level of risk the fund takes with its investments. If they are lucky and the increased risk pays off, the inflow from investments will increase and the company will not have to make any contributions for the time being. Even though these risky investments could turn sour, making the pension fund and plan participants worse off, some executives might be willing to "shoot the dice."

DUMPING GROUND FOR PERSONAL/CORPORATE EXPENSES

Only pension fund related expenses should ever be paid out of the pension fund. Legitimate expenses include pension fund staff salaries (while conducting pension fund business), investment management fees, consulting fees, brokerage expenses, pension fund related computer expenses, office supplies, and, sometimes, even office space. However, there is little to stop senior executives from taking advantage of the fund's resources for personal or corporate use.

Rank has its privileges, as the saying goes. The chief executive officer in one company asked the pension fund's chief investment officer to evaluate the investments in several portfolios of an outside foundation fund of which he was a trustee. This fund had nothing to do with the company's pension fund; it was simply a personal, outside interest. Both the chief executive officer and the chief investment officer knew, or had reason to know by virtue of their positions, that a personal study that uses pension fund resources is a violation of ERISA.

To be fair, the chief executive officer may have felt the foundation fund was a worthwhile commitment of his time, and it may have been. Moreover, he may have believed the cost to do the evaluations would be small. He may also have felt it was his right as chief executive officer to use lower-level people in whatever way he saw fit. But his motivation for making the request is not the point. ERISA states that the resources of the pension fund are to be used *solely* in the interests of plan participants.

When the project was turned over to the pension fund staff member who would actually have to do the work, he balked. He reminded the chief investment officer that the study would require pension fund resources and his salary was paid out of the pension fund. The chief investment officer would have none of it, however, and demanded the analysis be done, quickly and thoroughly, or else.

The staff member completed the analysis as ordered. It required the use of a sophisticated computer program provided by a pension fund supplier. The program was run several times exclusively for this review; the results were analyzed and evaluated by pension fund personnel on pension fund time; and a detailed report was written, typed, and given to the chief investment officer to forward to the chief executive officer. The review was estimated to cost the pension fund several thousands of dollars.

Much later, the issue of the propriety of the chief executive officer's special study came to the attention of the company's board of directors — specifically the board member whose committee supervised the company's pension fund investment activities. Technically at least, the chief executive officer reports to the board. The board member's conclusion was the special study was done at no "direct cost" to the pension fund or the company, and he found no inappropriate behavior involved. Even though the study cost the pension fund several thousands of dollars, he said it didn't and that was that.

Similar kinds of "corner-cutting" by highly paid executives go on every day. They are violations, yes, but are so much a part of the corporate culture they have become almost acceptable. Nevertheless, when it comes to the pension fund, these culturally "acceptable" activities are unacceptable. It's not a cultural issue, it's a legal issue — pension fund assets and resources are to be used solely for the benefit of plan participants. Furthermore, if this type of activity is allowed, where does it stop? Is requisitioning several thousands of dollars of pension fund resources by senior executives acceptable, but not pocketing $50,000 in cash? Finally, once a company condones small transgressions like a chief executive officer's special study, plan participants are eventually headed for trouble. This type of thing has a tendency to snowball. It encourages a whole attitude shift that allows other, much more harmful transgressions to become just a way of doing business.

Another example involves charging corporate expenses to the pension fund. Say the chief investment officer is nervous and wants some help responding to questions raised by a persistent, knowledgeable newspaper reporter. One approach a chief investment officer might take is to hire a media relations firm to provide assistance. The resulting consultations, which could include role-playing and videotaping, might cost about $10,000. Although the chief investment officer pays the bill out of the pension fund, it seems the chief investment officer and the company benefit from this exercise, not plan participants. Yet the pension fund picks up the tab, not the company. Doesn't seem right, does it?

Moreover, it is doubtful that anyone on the outside will ever know about the transaction. The only information a pension fund is legally bound to provide plan participants is a copy of the fund's Form 5500 Report (plus some trustee-related documents), which the company must file every year with the IRS and the Department of Labor. Anyone reviewing those documents would see that $10,000 was paid by the pension fund to a media company. That's all. Unless someone knew the story behind the expenditure they wouldn't have any idea what it was for, and the company is not required to provide any more information.

This lack of detailed information can extend to other expenditures as well. Say a pension fund is under investigation by the Department of Labor. The company hires some top-notch legal experts to defend its interests and perhaps its senior executives. Hundreds of thousands of dollars in legal fees are racked up. Should these expenses be charged to the pension fund, or are they really a corporate expenditure and thus chargeable to the company? Just try to find out the details from a company determined to keep things quiet. The Form 5500 Report will only list the names of the law firms and what they were paid. It does not itemize the bills, and, as in the example of the media consultant, the company can refuse to provide a plan participant with any additional information.

So senior executives can use the pension fund to pay for corporate or personal projects without anyone on the outside knowing about it. An investigator looking in wouldn't have a clue as to what went on.

MISUSE OF PRIVATE INFORMATION

In the course of the job, a chief investment officer can become privy to a lot of money-making information. For example, investment bankers make the rounds of the pension funds looking for financing for their mergers and acquisitions. When they make their presentations, they stress the deal's profit potential. However, if they want to improve their chances of getting a loan from the pension fund they normally would have to reveal the details of the takeover — including the price they are going to offer for the target company's common stock. This bid price can be 25 to 30 percent higher than what the stock is currently trading for. If the investment bankers don't reveal the amount they intend to bid, the chief investment officer can easily estimate it by carefully analyzing the presentation material. Even if the price is not revealed, just knowing a takeover is seriously being considered is enough to make some money.

The bid price and other takeover information is private, non-public information and should not be used for personal gain. Still, a chief investment officer could covertly use that information to make lots of money. All he or she has to do is to buy the call options on the target company's stock before the investment banker makes the bid public. Call options give the buyer a right to purchase shares over a specified time period at a specified price. Using options, a chief investment officer could easily triple his or her money when the bid was later made public.

A clever chief investment officer, however, would not take advantage of this information personally. If the trading activity leading up to the announcement was researched, the chief investment officer's name could appear. Sure, the chief investment officer might be able to hide behind some trust account, but why take the chance that even this tactic would not be enough of a cover? It is simply safer for the chief investment officer to tip off friends about the intended acquisition — friends who would later be expected to do something nice for the chief investment officer.

How much money could be involved? Consider some of the insider trading cases that have recently hit the press. One involved the takeover of Motel 6 by a French company. It was alleged that $4.5 million in illegal profits were made by individuals who bought the securities based on insider information before the acquisition was announced. Another insider trading case involved a merger. Apparently a consultant for a human resources firm that was hired in connection with confidential merger discussions tipped off a neighbor about the pending deal. The neighbor purchased the securities and allegedly pocketed $255,000 in trading profits. Another involved a law firm retained by a client in merger and acquisition work. The National Association of Securities Dealers was looking into unusual trading patterns in the stock of a company who was a client. Lo and behold, the name of the brother of one of the lawyers appeared on the list of individuals who traded in the stock before the deal was announced. These examples did not involve insider trading by pension fund personnel, but to think the opportunity doesn't exist within a pension fund is naive.

Another example of profiting from the information that comes across a chief investment officer's desk involves the personal contacts the chief investment officer has cultivated using pension fund assets. For example, it just might be mentioned to a chief investment officer by one of these contacts that this person's company is thinking about making an acquisition of another company. This is money-making information. In one such case, the chief investment officer and selected friends bought the stock options on the takeover candidate. Sure enough, news of the possible takeover was later rumored in the press, and the shares increased and the price of the options nearly doubled in one day.

Another, more commonplace source of money-making information is to "front run" the trades the pension fund is about to make. In other words, if there is a chance that the pension fund's investment activities will drive up the price of a particular security, a chief investment officer can reap a profit by making his or her purchases before the pension fund starts its trading activity. Often, a steady stream of transactions cross the chief investment officer's desk, so he or she need only pick those with the greatest opportunity for personal profit.

DOUBLE DIPPING

Double dipping involves getting paid twice for the same services. The easiest investment alternative for a chief investment officer to engage in this activity is in venture capital investments. For example, a chief investment officer can insist on becoming a director of either the venture capitalist's board of directors, the partnership's board of directors, and/or the young company's board. As a paid board member, the chief investment officer could pocket the director's fee even though he or she was on the pension fund's time. One pension fund staff member naively suggested to a chief investment officer that it just didn't seem right that anyone who collected a salary from the pension fund should also accept a fee from one of the fund's investment managers even if it was compensation to serve on a board of directors. The chief investment officer reportedly burst out laughing and said that many senior executives sit on the boards of other companies — and get paid to do so even though technically they are on their own company's payroll at the time. He was right, of course, but pension fund employees should be held to a higher standard than "normal" corporate practices. Accepting money for a directorship with a pension fund supplier could be viewed as a quid pro quo. Moreover, objectivity could be compromised when the investment manager's performance was being evaluated.

A second source of double dipping is from expense reimbursements. Normally, board members are reimbursed for the expenses they incur to attend a meeting. Airfare, hotel, meals, and taxi fares could amount to several hundreds of dollars. But a chief investment officer can arrange some other pension fund business in the same town and request reimbursement of expenses from the pension fund, then pocket the check received from the investment manager. It's not big money, but with several board memberships which meet several times a year, the chief investment officer could end up with an extra $15,000 to $20,000 annually.

An auditor might catch on if the chief investment officer became a board member for a venture capital partnership in which the pension fund had just invested a big chuck of money. To counter that, a clever chief investment officer would become a director in another partnership offered by the same venture capitalist, but one in which the pension fund had not invested any money. In such cases it would take a lot of digging to uncover the connection.

POLITICAL INFLUENCE

A two-month investigation into local and state public pension funds concluded:

The unsettling results: [These public] pension funds all are giving lucrative contracts to firms that help finance the campaigns of the
politicians who have influence over the pension funds . . . In some
cases, the firms made political donations and later received a money
management contract; in others, the firms first received the contract
and then began making contributions . . . Campaign contributions are
the most quantifiable aspect of the multifaceted relationship between
pols and the managers. But it's the mix of sometimes modest contributions, coupled with political connections and clout-heavy friend-
ships, that fosters a cozy relationship between politicians and money
managers.

. . . [I]n several cases, the money managers have been mediocre or
poor performers. In others, the firms had minimal track records when
they were hired. And critics say some were hired without a thorough
examination of other managers.

At best, the situation represents a potential conflict of interest for
the politicians. At worst, it provides a systematic opportunity to reward political allies at the expense of taxpayers and pensioners.[11]

This type of thing can also go on in a corporate pension fund.
For example, perhaps some important legislation is pending that af-
fects the company or its industry, or some committee is meeting and
the company wants to get a lawmaker's ear. An investment manager
might be known to have the necessary political contacts. If senior executives wanted this investment manager hired, they will get their
way, even if it is over the bodies of the pension fund staff members
who object.

COOKING PERFORMANCE NUMBERS

Good performance numbers can do a lot for a chief investment officer's career. Certainly, they can improve outside marketability, but
more than that they can improve inside esteem. Once a chief investment officer has built up the confidence of senior management, he or
she is likely to be given more leeway. Approval of investment decisions becomes easier, and indiscretions might be overlooked because
senior management doesn't want to lose this "investment genius."
Good performance numbers can also do a lot for the chief investment

---

11. "Illinois Public Funds Hire Political Players — Campaign Donors End Up Getting Business," *Pension & Investments*, August 22, 1994.

officer's own pocketbook. Some pension funds have at least one component of compensation tied to the pension fund's performance.

Making a pension fund's performance look better than it really is is not too difficult. It involves squeezing out as much performance as possible from the pension fund by upward inflating assets that do not have a readily available market price, such as real estate and venture capital, and picking the benchmark that is easiest to beat against which to compare the pension fund's inflated results.

Let's start with the benchmark first. One of the most commonly used comparisons is the performance of other, similar funds. If your pension fund is beating a group of other pension funds, then the perception is that the chief investment officer must be doing a pretty good job. But the question is, which other pension funds are included in the benchmark, and who makes that decision?

All pension funds are unique; they differ in size, objectives, and plan participants. The biggest difference is between public pension funds, which are supported by a governmental group, and private pension funds, which are supported by a company. Public pension funds often have various investment restrictions placed on them. Some might be allowed to invest only up to a certain percentage in common stock; others are excluded from investing in international securities; and still others are restricted in some other way. Whether these restrictions are appropriate is not the issue; what is important is the fact that they exist. A clever chief investment officer can take advantage of those restrictions in biasing the benchmark against which his or her pension fund is to be measured. For example, consider international investments, which have done very well over the last five to ten years. If a public fund is prohibited from investing in those markets, its performance is likely to be less than that of a private pension fund with a large exposure to international issues. If those public funds then are included in a benchmark, the benchmark's return would be lower than if it included only private pension funds. So, by juggling what goes into a benchmark, a clever chief investment officer can construct a performance number that is relatively easy to beat in a specific time frame. Since the calculations of the benchmark are done after the fact, it is relatively easy to pick and choose what components go into the benchmark.

The next step in cooking performance results is to inflate the pension fund's reported performance. The easiest way to do this is by

re-valuing upward the fund's real estate and venture capital investments. Unlike common stocks, an investor cannot open a newspaper
and find daily trading prices for major real estate holdings. A piece of
real estate's true worth is unknown until the property is sold. In the
meantime, appraisers are hired to assign a "value" to the property. In
some cases, the chief investment officer might turn the appraisal job
over to a member of his or her own staff, then encourage that person
to be generous with the assessment. Therein lies the conflict. Consider this:

> Prudential Insurance Co. of America conceded it had improperly in-
> flated the value of two real-estate funds it sold to pension funds . . .
> Yesterday's disclosures resulted from an extensive internal investiga-
> tion that was prompted by a lawsuit, filed last fall in New Jersey Su-
> perior Court in Newark, by Mark Jorgensen, formerly manager for
> three of Prudential's real-estate funds. He charged the company with
> demoting him after he complained that the company was inflating re-
> turns and increasing the fees on one of the funds, the Prudential
> Property Investment Separate Account, known as Prisa . . . Previ-
> ously, Prudential had insisted that Mr. Jorgensen's charges were
> groundless and stemmed from his unhappiness about being demoted
> after a reorganization.[12]

This is not an isolated case. One real estate investment advisor
told investors a Los Angeles office building was worth $265 million at
the end of 1993, yet in the first quarter of 1994 another appraiser val-
ued it at $160 million.[13] That is a 65 percent difference in appraised
value in just one quarter!

This is not to say all appraisals are useless or are biased and val-
ueless. However, if a chief investment officer wants to cook performance results, the means to inflate the pension fund's performance are
available. Senior management's eyes might glaze over when the discussion turns to how returns are calculated and the pros and cons of
using specific benchmarks. A chief investment officer can also assume
that no one will check the numbers, and to add a degree of comfort,
he or she could ask a friendly consultant to report the numbers to the
investment policy committee.

---

12. "Prudential Says It Inflated the Value of 2 Realty Funds, Asks Aides to Quit," *The Wall Street Journal*, April 29, 1994.
13. "Building Value Questioned," *Pension & Investments*, August 22, 1994.

With an inflated pension fund return and a benchmark that is lower than it should be, a chief investment officer might look like an investment genius. A self-serving chief investment officer could easily paint a picture that does not match reality if the investment policy committee lacks street smarts.

REPUTATION-ENHANCING MOVES

A chief investment officer can enhance his or her esteem with senior management in many ways. Doing an outstanding job and turning in good performance is the best way for plan participants. However, as was shown in the last section it is easy for a chief investment officer to give the perception of good results by cooking the performance numbers.

Another way to enhance esteem is to have people praise you. Generating undeserved favorable comments from others is not difficult. Once again it turns on the power of money — lots of money. At its most basic, this is just one of the tactics used by an "old boy" network: You do something good for me (give me a contract worth millions in fees), and I'll do something good for you (in this case pass along favorable comments to senior management, which might help your career). It is unlikely that an investment manager who was collecting $1 million a year in management fees would bad-mouth his or her benefactor. At the minimum, they would remain silent for fear of any negative comments getting back to the chief investment officer and damaging the relationship. If they did share the bad news with anyone, it would probably be among just a few close colleagues.

A clever chief investment officer will not intentionally use pension fund suppliers to deliver the favorable comments, however. That is too obvious. Senior executives might correctly reason that these remarks are biased. A better source is someone senior management trusts and who on the surface does not appear to have anything to gain from the comments. For example, senior management might have established a good working relationship with certain investment bankers. Investment bankers advise a company about mergers and acquisitions, arrange financing, and help a company with other financial matters. On the surface there seems to be no contact with the pension fund. However, the investment banking firm often is part of a larger firm, which also has a brokerage subsidiary. It is the brokerage subsidiary that might do a substantial amount of business with the pension fund and thus wants the investment bankers to pass along favorable comments about the chief investment officer. Far-fetched? Just remember, there are millions of dollars of business on the line.

Supplying senior executives with favorable comments occurs even before a chief investment officer is hired. Senior executives will often ask pension fund suppliers about candidates for an open chief investment officer position. Higher management thinks they are getting valuable input, and, depending upon who they talk to, the advice could in fact be good.

Some pension fund suppliers, however, will use the opportunity to get a leg up on the competition. They will offer up the name of someone who might feel obligated to them for their help in getting them the job. The lobbying effort by pension fund suppliers for the candidate of their choice can be very intense. All of the supplier's contacts with the company might be pressed into action — even contacts that are totally unrelated to the pension fund. And the supplier will let the prospective candidate know all about the supplier's efforts to secure the position for the individual.

Sadly, the opposite is true as well. If a candidate was expected to threaten an account relationship, it is very doubtful that an investment manager would pass along favorable comments. Finally, if a staff member was threatening an account relationship, a manager can be expected to do whatever it takes to get that person removed.

INCREASING THE RISK LEVEL OF PENSION FUND INVESTMENTS

A chief investment officer could manipulate the mix of investments in the pension fund for his or her own personal advantage. Since balancing risk with return is a subjective decision, a set of assumptions could be easily constructed that can bias the pension fund's mix of investments toward a particular type of investment. This chicanery could be of advantage to a chief investment officer who sees his or her next job in that area. By having lots of money to spread around he or she can collect a lot of IOUs from investment managers and could establish some important personal contacts. The downside for plan participants is this intentional bias toward one investment type increases the fund's risk exposure.

Another reason a chief investment officer might be motivated to play games with the asset mix is to take advantage of a performance-based compensation package. For example, if a chief investment officer's pay is based on how well a fund has performed, there might be a temptation to skew the asset mix toward investments that have the potential for very high returns. If they hit, the chief investment officer might get paid a bigger bonus. However, with the expectation for high returns comes very high risk exposure. If the risky investments turn sour, well, it wasn't the chief investment officer's money anyway.

As argued previously, performance-based compensation at every level makes sense. Senior management must be very careful, however, in constructing these packages so they do not inadvertently include an incentive for the chief investment officer to "roll the dice" with investments. One way to avoid this pitfall is to pay for long-term results.

Surely, the investment policy committee or the pension investment committee of the board of directors must approve any changes in the asset mix? They will screen out risky investment alternatives. Perhaps — but consider the plight of one small Texas college that invested its long-term investment funds in volatile mortgage-based derivatives:

> ... [T]he college has been brutally punished. Officials say [the college's] investment portfolio, purchased for $21.9 million, has lost almost half its value since January. The decline, according to administrators, has more than wiped out the previous years' gains.
>
> The college, unable to pay its bills, has been forced to borrow $10.5 million on an emergency basis, has increased tuition 20% and has raised real-estate taxes on local property owners 7.2%. At the same time, it has slashed its operating budget to $16 million from $18 million. Twenty-two senior professors have been given early retirement to save $850,000 in salaries, and [the college] president for 20 years, is forgoing his $122,500 salary. Faculty travel has been all but eliminated.[14]

People on pension fund investment committees may not understand pension fund investments or may be so preoccupied with running the business that they just might leave all the decisions to a

---

14. "I Owe U — How a Texas College Mortgaged Its Future in Derivatives Debacle," *The Wall Street Journal*, September 23, 1994.

risk-taking chief investment officer. Consider the Orange County example:

> To the untrained eye, Orange County's portfolio didn't look particularly risky. It mainly consisted of high-quality bonds issued by U.S. government-sponsored agencies, with relatively modest maturities of five years or less . . . But those innocuous-looking holdings were leveraged 3-to-1 through repurchase agreements with Wall Street firms. Like normal margin accounts, reverse repurchases involve buying securities with borrowed money, with the securities pledged as collateral . . . The repurchase arrangements amplify investors' returns and risks.[15]

On the other hand, senior executives might actually encourage risk-taking in the pension fund. Higher pension fund returns could mean the company's contribution could be lowered or even eliminated, which would cause earnings and executive compensation to increase. Because investment policy decisions are not generally shared with plan participants, no one would be the wiser.

15. "Bitter Fruit — Orange County, Mired in Investment Mess, Files for Bankruptcy," *The Wall Street Journal*, January 7, 1994.

CHAPTER 9

The Challenge of
Disclosing Chicanery

Even if some of the activities described in the two previous chapters are not illegal, certainly they seem unlikely to benefit the pension fund. If these activities are to be stopped or at least slowed down, the underlying environment that allows them to be hidden from view needs to be addressed. That is the topic of this chapter.

COLLATERAL BENEFITS

A chief investment officer places pension fund money into a venture with a well-known celebrity. Sure, approval might have occurred outside the normal routine, and the fees, the personal service contract, and the price paid are a bit steep, but on the surface nothing else seems unusual or out of line. Money is invested; the deal is done.

But what are the collateral benefits? Perhaps the chief investment officer harbored a desire to start an investment management firm, which would cater to high-net-worth individuals. So, along with the investment the chief investment officer gets a collateral benefit — a name or contact which might be of personal use in the future.

Scores of people use their jobs to network, but what if the real reason for making the investment and providing excellent terms to the partner was *just* to get that contact? In other words, establishing a contact with a specific individual was not a collateral benefit, but instead was the real reason the deal was done in the first place.

Someone from the outside looking in would have a tough time ferreting out what really went on, much less proving it. Short of having the chief investment officer's voice on tape saying the real reason the investment was made was because he or she wanted to gain an entry into the high-net-worth marketplace, an outside investigator might not even suspect what was going on. The chief investment officer could be expected to hide the truth, and if senior management even suspected the real reason, it is unlikely they would tell the pension fund's trustees or an outside investigator. Maybe the senior executives were lax in their due diligence and this "investment" lost a bundle. Not wanting to be embarrassed or lose their jobs, senior management might just prefer to cover-up the mess by casting the deal as a poor investment decision. Case closed.

Another example involves pension fund expense money instead of a pension fund investment. Say the chief investment officer and a senior executive wanted to see The Masters golf tournament in Georgia but didn't want to pay for the trip themselves. One way to get what they want is to arrange a trip to visit a pension fund investment manager or some of the pension fund's real estate investments in Atlanta. Since this is pension fund "business," the airfare and other expenses can be charged to the pension fund. Entrance to the tournament could be provided by a pension fund supplier. An outside investigator thumbing through stacks of expense vouchers might see the expenses associated with the trip and would never suspect that a side trip to Augusta had occurred or that the golf outing was the real reason for the trip.

The golf outing could be effectively hidden from view. If someone does challenge the expenses, the chief investment officer and the senior executive will assert that the purpose of the trip was to visit the investment manager or the real estate property. They could be expected to say the golf outing was the collateral benefit, not the real reason for the trip. Absent a tape recording, no one could prove otherwise. Another case closed.

These examples illustrate how easy it is to get away with wrongdoing in a pension fund by simply casting the activity in a different light.

SENIOR MANAGEMENT INVOLVEMENT

Another possibility that would allow questionable activities to continue undiscovered in a pension fund is when senior management is involved. They might just have their own hands in the pension fund cookie jar.

Senior executives might use the assets and resources of the pension fund to advance corporate or personal goals. They can be involved in fiddling with assumptions so that the plan's liabilities look lower than they really are; hiring investment managers because of their political contacts; becoming a trustee of a mutual fund that is managed by a broker who does millions of dollars of business with the pension fund; using the pension fund's clout to get a retiring executive a job; using pension fund suppliers for tickets to sporting and cultural events; and hiring venture capital firms to get a window on technology that will help the company with its own products and services.

Since senior executives are in charge of hiring and firing pension fund employees, rest assured they can get just about anything they want — even if it takes several reorganizations and "careful" selection of a new chief investment officer to get it. With the "proper" personnel in place, any amount of data can be generated to "justify" any senior executive decision with no fear of detection.

In an environment where senior executives do not live up to their responsibilities, legal or ethical, wrongdoing can run rampant and could go on for a very long time indeed. Moreover, they have the tools to hide their activities from the trustees, and, indeed, some trustees might even be involved.

CHIEF INVESTMENT
OFFICER INVOLVEMENT

Another instance when wrongdoing can go undetected for a long time occurs when the pension fund has an especially clever chief investment officer. Such a person just might be able to convince senior executives into thinking he or she is something they are not and, in the process, pick the pension fund's pocket.

First, the chief investment officer must create an appearance of competency. That's easy to do by changing the pension fund's assumptions to reduce corporate contributions, cooking performance numbers, working with pension fund suppliers to provide positive feedback to senior executives, and restricting staff contact with higher management.

Next, the chief investment officer must keep his or her staff off balance. That too is easy to do by hand-picking one's own staff members, eliminating staff meetings so no one knows specifically what the others are doing, constantly reorganizing the group, and enticing staff members into engaging in questionable activities themselves.

Third, the chief investment officer needs to gain control over the fees paid to suppliers as this is the grease that makes the wheels go around smoothly. This he or she can do by paying as much of the expenses as possible out of the pension fund rather than the company's budget (out of sight, out of mind), lowering expenses on some items to give more leeway on others, and making ample use of soft dollar arrangements.

Fourth, the chief investment officer must carefully structure self-serving investments and personal deals. This can be done by mixing in only a few self-serving scams a year, structuring the deals as judgment calls, picking investments whose true return won't be known for years and whose current market valuations are hard to come by, approaching each committee member for their approval individually instead of in a group meeting, and by controlling the investment policy committee agenda and flow of information.

Finally, the chief investment officer must do whatever senior management wants regardless of his or her fiduciary responsibilities. How can senior executives later complain when the chief investment officer puts his or her hand in the cookie jar, if theirs is already in it?

If a clever chief investment officer does these things, he or she could milk the pension fund for years.

FEAR OF RETALIATION

Wrongdoing can go on undetected in a pension fund for a prolonged time period. Is it really undetected, though? Doesn't someone on staff sense what is going on and become disgusted with it? Perhaps, yet they might not come forward because they are fearful of retaliation. It would take an exceptional individual to knowingly sacrifice himself or herself for a concept as diffuse as "the interests of plan participants."

It is far easier to avoid the hassle and damage to one's career and look the other way, or move on to another, more ethical environment.

Typically, the first reaction a whistle-blower will receive is to be ignored. But since wrongdoing is like an iceberg — much of it is below the surface — a whistle-blower may have unknowingly stumbled onto a larger problem. Other senior executives might have been involved or, at least embarrassed, by what went on. Now their careers and reputations are on the line. These executives, by virtue of their rank within the company, are survivors of corporate political warfare. They know how to hurt someone, and badly. Retaliation is likely to be swift and brutal. First, pressure will be put on the individual to drop the complaint. This can take several forms, including senior executives putting their own spin on events and trying to convince the whistle-blower that he or she didn't see the big picture. This "drop the complaint" step is especially effective if the whistle-blower was foolish enough to report the wrongdoing to someone within his or her own chain of command. Those people will try to do whatever they can to contain and neutralize the allegations, perhaps even resorting to blackmail by threatening to tell the public what the whistle-blower revealed in confidence.

Next, the whistle-blower can expect to have his or her duties limited and, perhaps, even be transferred to another, lower-level position or some distant outpost. "Demands of the job," senior executives will explain. It is likely the individual's performance reviews will turn poor, and he or she will be defamed. Some executives might try to refocus the investigation on why the whistle-blower came forward.

Finally, at some point the whistle-blower will resign or be fired. It is sometimes difficult, psychologically, for co-workers and potential employers to accept that a company will retaliate against a whistle-blower. It violates their perceptions of a "just world." They are more likely to believe that there is more to the story than pure retaliation, that the whistle-blower must have gotten what he or she deserved. The whistle-blower's earnings prospects could be diminished.

The former whistle-blowing employee could file a lawsuit, but the way things stand in some states he or she would have to prove some legal basis. In some states employees fall under an "employment-at-will" doctrine. Essentially this says that, absent an employment contract, the company has the right to fire an employee at any time, with or without cause. The rationale companies use to defend the "employment-at-will" doctrine is that, because an employee is free to terminate his or her employment at any time, with or without cause or notice, the company should be allowed to do the same with respect to its employees.

Collective bargaining agreements have narrowed the scope of the doctrine for union employees, and laws have prohibited discharging someone on the basis of race, gender, religion, age, national origin, or handicaps. Certainly, a company needs to have the flexibility to dismiss nonperforming employees or to initiate layoffs when there is not enough work for even the most outstanding of employees. But retaliation firings? That's another story. Sadly, if a pension fund employee tells senior management about questionable activities in the pension fund which involve senior executives, he or she risks being terminated. The company's lawyers will just claim the firing was performance related and then hide behind the "employment-at-will" doctrine.

One company produced a code of business conduct document which, according to one lawyer, was not worth the paper it was printed on. It stated:

> Employees who report irregularities in good faith will not be disciplined nor subject to any retaliation as a result of such a report.

On the surface this sounds like a commitment. However, the document also had a section on the "employment-at-will" doctrine to make sure it was understood that the company did not relinquish its rights to terminate someone with or without cause. Further weakening the above statement, the company concluded its written code with the statement that the code was neither a contract of employment nor a guarantee of continuing company policy.

Individuals who decide to pursue a lawsuit against a company for its retaliatory behavior must realize that the deck is stacked against them. The company undoubtedly has a well-financed legal department. They know the system and how to use it to their advantage, especially if the legal basis for the claim is not well established. As this might be the first time the individual has ever been involved in a lawsuit, he or she will be bewildered by the legal maneuvers and cost. If the company does not have the legal talent on staff, they certainly can hire the best. They have the resources to outlast, outspend, and outlitigate an individual. Think of the disruption that years of costly litigation will have on a person's family and finances.

A contingency fee attorney might help. These lawyers work for a percentage of the settlement, if there is one. Fees vary, but often the arrangement is for one-third. Sometimes a retainer has to be put up, against which the attorney can draw. Getting a top-notch contingency fee attorney to pursue a whistle-blowing case might be difficult if the case appears likely to turn into a long, drawn out affair — which, of course, the company will try to make it. This type of case is a battle of attrition.

Besides the financial burden, there are other disincentives for legal action. The major one is the potential damage to the individual's career and reputation. The company will undoubtedly portray the whistle-blower as the worst employee who ever worked for that company. It is doubtful that any of the company's investment managers, consultants, or other suppliers will come to the whistle-blower's aid. They have their own families and futures to protect — as well as millions of dollars in fees. Indeed, those outside organizations who were involved directly or indirectly in the wrongdoing will relish the opportunity to dump on the whistle-blower.

Some antiretaliation protection is provided pension fund employees by federal law if they go to the Department of Labor with their allegations. But that's the key: They must go to the Department of Labor. However, even if they do there still is nothing to prevent a company from transferring that person to some distant outpost or just waiting awhile and firing him or her later. In short, there are plenty of ways to make life rough for the whistle-blower if senior management wishes to do so.

Given the guns a vindictive senior executive can aim at a pension fund employee, can you really fault some people for just looking the other way?[1]

COVER-UP

If the questionable activities involve or implicate the most senior executives of the company, they can be expected to take action to protect themselves. The first, most likely step is to hire an outside law firm to "investigate" the allegations of wrongdoing. This gives the appearance

---

1. Note: See Marcia Miceli and Janet Near, *Blowing the Whistle*, Lexington Books, 1992, for a thorough discussion of retaliation.

of concern and the facade of an independent investigation. But chances are good the selection will not be just any old law firm; the decision is likely to be a cold and calculating one. The "ideal" law firm will have done lots of business with the company over the years, and perhaps even with the pension fund. Moreover, the senior partners at the law firm will have known the company's senior executives for years. Unfortunately, some lawyers might think that since they were hired by the senior executives, they have an allegiance to them rather than to the pension plan's trustees, the company, and its shareowners.

> When faced with possible wrongdoing these days, many companies quickly call in a prominent lawyer as special counsel. The attorney investigates, then reports to a special committee of the board . . . But the practice remains controversial. No matter how much integrity the lawyers have, outsiders remain aware that the lawyers are investigating their own clients. As the old saying goes: "Who pays the piper calls the tune."[2]

This does not necessarily mean the law firm would deliberately cover up illegal acts. No reputable lawyer would do that — but having a lawyer doing something that would jeopardize his or her license is not really necessary. Rather it is the company's senior executives who can control the depth, scope, and outcome of the investigation. Here is how.

Investigations cost money. The hourly billing for just two of the law firm's partners could run $500 to $1,000 per hour. Several weeks of questioning people, and perhaps retaining a private investigator or two, and the total cost could be in the range of several hundreds of thousands of dollars. The senior executives could use this cost factor as an excuse to limit the scope of the investigation to lower level management activities. Presto, the senior executives are out of the line of fire.

A lower level employee who points the finger upward can be handled in several ways. Paper trails at the senior executive's level could be hard to come by, and without these documents proof is difficult. Consider this comment by a senior executive: "Having been sued . . . 55 times or more, my files are relatively clean."

Even if there is a paper trail, senior executives, and even trustees, can put a favorable spin on events. Consider the board member, who

2. "Who Pays the Piper . . . ," *Forbes*, February 15, 1993.

was also a trustee, who claimed the chief executive officer's special study did not incur any "direct costs." No cost, no violation, was the conclusion.

Even if senior executives can't control the investigation, there is a built-in advantage for those who are going to be investigated in being able to select the investigator. Whether a particular action is illegal or just poor judgment is often a gray area. Hand-picked lawyers might be willing to give the senior executives the benefit of the doubt. For example, a senior executive directing the pension fund to hire a specific manager might be poor judgment, but not illegal unless there was some kickback or quid pro quo. Hand-picked lawyers might say "tut-tut, poor judgment," but find no evidence of wrongdoing. They may be relieved that a cursory examination revealed nothing and then quickly move on.

Finally, getting the lawyers involved in the investigation means that later, should someone ask for information, the reply could be: "Sorry, that information is protected by client/attorney privilege." The law, quite rightly, protects the communication between a client and his or her attorney. A crafty senior executive team would know that and use it to its advantage.

After hiring a "friendly" law firm, the next step would be to remove any witnesses so that no one will be looking over the company's shoulders pointing out embarrassing connections. Scattering certain staff members also makes it extremely difficult, time consuming, and expensive for any other investigator to uncover anything. The ex-staff members could still testify, but it is not likely that they will appear voluntarily. Most will just want to get on with their lives. Getting involved in a sticky legal situation might jeopardize current or future employment, so why bother?

The next step senior executives might take is to clean up all the records. All the files could be put in pristine shape. There is no need to keep the old documents because now the fund has current ones — at least that is an excuse someone could use if they were asked to produce the earlier files. No documents, no proof. The issue becomes one person's word against another.

Finally, another step senior executives might use in their cover-up campaign is to delay, delay, and delay. If questions come up very early, the standard response could be: "We are investigating that and can't comment at this time." When the questions come up again later, the response will be: "That's old news." At no time will any information or results be revealed. Delaying also helps since there is a statute of limitations on bringing legal action.

A modification of this delaying tactic involves giving the appearance of being forthcoming while stonewalling. This variation can take many forms. For example, if a lower level employee has done something wrong, the company might pursue that individual with vigor. It doesn't matter that a pass may have been given to a senior executive who engaged in a similar or worse transgression. Just hang the lower level person out to dry; then the company can say it took things seriously while ignoring action against those who were in charge of the process.

Unless trustees control the investigation right from the outset, with the selection of the investigators, senior executives have a huge advantage in making a cover-up a reality.

CHAPTER 10

The Way Things Should Be

This chapter outlines some actions trustees, as instruments of change, should take to protect the pension fund's assets and resources. These ideas won't automatically make the pension fund safe, but they are steps in the right direction.

STREAMLINE THE ORGANIZATIONAL STRUCTURE

The pension fund's decision-making structure could invite senior management abuse. Consider the sample organization structure described in Chapter 5. The chief investment officer reported to a treasurer, who reported to a chief financial officer, who reported to the chief executive officer, who reported to the board of directors. There was also an internal investment policy committee made up of senior company personnel, which reported to a pension investment committee of the board of directors.

Trustees should cut through all the layers of organization and reduce the opportunity for self-serving behavior. An organization is needed that clearly defines and focuses responsibilities. Starting at the top, the board of directors of some companies bury the pension fund's responsibilities in a board committee that has many other tasks. This is wrong, because it is too easy for the committee members to get involved in the other areas and thus shortchange the pension fund. It provides a ready excuse for busy board members to delegate pension fund responsibilities downward. Therefore, the first step is to change the structure such that a committee of the board of directors has as its only responsibility pension fund oversight.

Second, committee rules should require that members be completely free of potential conflicts of interest. At the minimum this means that they or their firms should be prohibited from doing any kind of business with the pension fund. The potential for conflict needs to be eliminated, and, indeed, the rule extended. Any member of the board of directors, whether on the pension fund committee or not, should not be allowed to have a business relationship with the pension fund, period. The idea behind these rule changes is to try and limit the opportunity for personal gain for those in power.

Third, the board committee should hire and have report directly to it an oversight consultant, the master trustee, and the auditors. Interviewing and selection should be done by committee members so there is no doubt that these individuals and/or organizations report to the committee. An oversight consultant's function is to provide feedback to the committee as to the methods and procedures of the pension fund, not to make investment decisions. It should be made clear to the consultant that he or she is not a surrogate chief investment officer, but rather has been hired to provide a sophisticated, auditing-like function. This would involve evaluating the calculation procedures and reviewing the results of pension fund performance numbers; evaluating the investment manager selection process; reviewing trading methods and results; and comparing the level of expenses, item by item, with other, similar pension funds. Presumably, this oversight consultant would have worked for years in the pension fund area and possess street smarts.

Fourth, in this ideal organization, the board committee should insist that an advisory board of outside investment professionals be established. This advisory board would act as a sounding board for proposed pension fund investment strategy and would provide a window on the investment environment. Members of the advisory board would concern themselves with macro investment decisions, such as the recommended asset mix and the proposed investment strategy for each of the investment types. They should not be involved in hiring or firing investment managers, nor should they have access to individual investment manager performance results. Focusing on macro investment issues is an attempt to minimize any potential for conflicts of interest among the outside advisors. For example, it doesn't make sense to have an investment manager making recommendations to hire or fire other investment managers. The opportunity for mutual backscratching is too great. Moreover, the advisory committee should act only in an advisory capacity.

To be more effective and focused, the advisory board should be relatively small, perhaps only five to six people including the chief investment officer. A limited number of staff members should be invited to attend meetings from time to time, and at least one of the members of the company's pension investment committee of the board of directors should be required to attend each meeting. Ideally, the advisory board should have one member as a professional expert representing each investment type; that is, one person who is experienced in common stock investments, another for bonds, another for real estate, and so forth. Meeting agendas should be established in consultation with the advisory board members and with the pension investment committee. Assignments for presentations should be given to the advisory board members, and meeting notes be kept and distributed to those company personnel involved in the pension fund investment process. If properly constructed and staffed, this advisory board would be an excellent resource, with which the trustees at the company and the chief investment officer could consult regarding their investment decisions.

Fifth, the chief investment officer and his or her staff should report directly to the pension investment committee of the board and to no one else. Having the chief investment officer and staff report directly to the committee reduces senior management's influence over pension assets.

Finally, retirees need to play a role in the decision-making process. They can be most effective as a member of the company's board of directors and chairman of the pension investment committee.

Figure 10–1 shows how the organization should look.

The purpose of this new alignment is to reduce the potential for any questionable use of pension fund resources by senior executives, to focus responsibility and sharpen accountability, and to give retirees a voice in the management of their pension fund's assets.

FIGURE   10–1

Suggested Organization

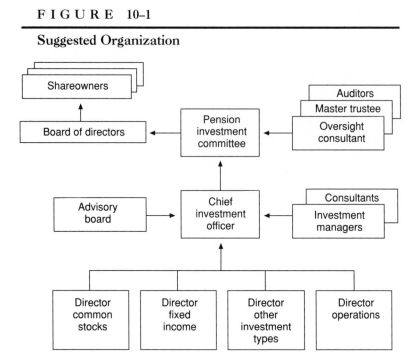

PROVIDE COMPLETE DISCLOSURE

The company is required to provide the government with certain information about its pension fund. Although plan participants have the right to see this information, it is difficult to read and virtually useless in assessing investment strategies or performance. Consider this excerpt from an editorial that appeared in a leading investment trade magazine:

> The 5500 annual report form filed by pension funds contains a lot of information, some of it probably even useful to the Labor Department. But it is impossibly complicated . . .[1]

If the investment professionals find these reports "impossibly complicated," as the editorial says, what chance does a plan participant have in deciphering what is going on?

---

1. "Time to Fix the 5500," editorial, *Pension and Investments*, January 10, 1994.

The details of what should be in an annual report to plan participants appear in Appendix 1 of this chapter. Briefly, the major areas that should be addressed in the report are:

- Asset allocation
- Investment strategy
- Funded status
- Performance results
- Expense information
- Issues and policy
- Ethics-related information
- Personnel-related information
- Signed actuarial report
- Signed auditor's report
- Signed trustee's report

The purpose of having this information is threefold. First, decisions that must be disclosed along with their results might motivate the decision makers to be a little more careful in making those decisions. Second, it gives plan participants the means to determine exactly how good of a job management is really doing with their pension fund. Finally, as a chief justice of the Supreme Court said, "sunshine is the best disinfectant."

Consider funded status. This section of the proposed annual report would reveal the size of the promises the company made to the plan's participants as compared to the amount of money in the pension fund. If a pension plan is underfunded (promises are larger than the amount of assets to pay for them), the company should explain in the annual report what is being done to correct the underfunding. Requiring the company to discuss this issue focuses attention on it. Plan participants should know how serious its senior management is about living up to the retirement promises they made.

Next, consider expense information. This section would reveal the size of investment management fees, consulting fees, brokerage commissions, and operating expenses. It would be in such detail that plan participants could see who got the money, how much, and what services were rendered. Aggregated salary paid to pension fund employees would also be included. Having to report expense information in this detail might motivate the company's decision makers to be more careful with how they spend the pension fund's money. It would also help stop the pension fund from being a dumping ground for corporate expenses. Also, because historical information should also be provided, plan participants will be able to easily see if expenses are getting out of hand.

Finally, consider asset allocation. This is the single most important investment decision those managing the pension fund's assets can make. It determines the risk level of the fund and most of its performance. This information should not be hidden from view.

Corporations produce detailed annual reports for shareowners and potential investors. Yet, although in some companies the size of the pension fund is over half the size of the market value of the company, no meaningful, readable annual report on pension fund activities is provided to plan participants. This is wrong. Clearly, pending or current pension fund transactions could be excluded if their disclosure might impact the financial outcome, but there is no justification for denying plan participants access to past decisions. In addition to a detailed annual report, plan participants should be allowed reasonable access to pension fund records and files. If reproduction/mailing cost is a problem, the company can make the report, records, and files available for review at company locations.

IMPROVE PENSION FUND AUDITS

Auditing a pension fund is a complex task. First, what is to be audited — investments, expenses, and/or investment manager fees? How frequently and in what depth? Who does the audit — the company's internal auditors, the pension fund's consultants, outside auditing firms, or various governmental agencies?

First, consider the internal auditing staff. One company's internal auditing staff reportedly spends about 90 percent of its time looking for ways to improve corporate earnings by simplifying jobs and duties. It's called "value-added auditing." That's a noble goal, but it also means that internal auditors are spending only 10 percent of their time on the old-fashioned type of auditing, which is designed to discourage people from engaging in activities they weren't supposed to get involved in. This company went even further — to emphasize the value-added aspects of the auditor's job, management tied the auditing department's bonus pool to the amount of corporate earnings they generated.

Value-added auditing is a good idea, but the old-fashioned variety can get short-changed right at the time it seems that fraud is on the increase. This is a dangerous combination. Look at Barings Brothers, Britain's oldest merchant bank, which reportedly lost $1 billion and, as a result, self-destructed:

> Why did Barings not tumble to Mr. Leeson's [apparently unauthorized trading] activities before it was too late? One answer is that nobody was watching him closely . . . Astonishingly, the bank did not require him to give up his job as head of settlements when he became head of trading . . . Allowing a trader to settle his own deals makes it simpler for him to hide the risks he is taking, or the amounts of money he is losing . . . "There was no control system," says a former colleague; "Nick was the system."[2]

Governmental groups, such as the Department of Labor and the IRS, also do audits of pension plans, but let's face reality. They can be strapped for resources. There are thousands of plans, and just a few hundred investigators. That leaves us with consultants and external auditors. Here, incredibly, senior executives might even allow the chief investment officer to select the auditor. Sure, an audit will be done, but apparently it doesn't dawn on some senior executives that, with a wink here and a nudge there, a chief investment officer, who controls the hiring and firing of the auditor, can narrow the audit's scope and depth — so much so that its usefulness is compromised.

There are some common-sense procedures that apply to the auditing function. For instance, the pension investment committee of the company's board of directors, not the chief investment officer, should select the pension fund's oversight consultant. Moreover, it is just plain common sense to rotate the oversight consulting assignment every couple of years so as to minimize the chance of cozy relationships finding root.

This is not to say that the chief investment officer should be subordinated to the consulting firm. The author has a problem with giving an outside consultant line officer's authority. Besides, it does not make much sense to hire a chief investment officer and then undercut his or her authority with a consultant. However, skillful trustees can,

---

2. "The Collapse of Barings — A Fallen Star," *The Economist*, March 4, 1995.

and should, walk the line between giving a chief investment officer responsibility and authority over investment decisions and allowing an oversight consultant to provide input in establishing investment control, ethical monitoring, and performance evaluation.

Second, the company should establish clear guidelines for pension fund policies and procedures. These would range from steps for approval and execution of investment decisions to operational matters. For example, the company should insist investment managers, consultants, and other pension fund suppliers disclose any finder fees that were paid to get the pension fund account and to whom. That's common sense.

Third, the company should make sure that at least one person on its internal auditing staff has a great deal of experience with pension fund investments. Ideally that individual will have street smarts and know where the skeletons can be hidden.

Fourth, annual audits of the entire pension fund operation by an independent, external accounting firm should be undertaken at the company's expense. The selected firm would be as neutral a party as is practical. To that end, the selected firm should not be the same firm that does the company's books and should have not any ties to senior management. The pension investment committee of the board of directors, not the chief investment officer, should make the selection with input provided by the company's accounting staff. Instructions to the auditing firm should be to do an old-fashioned audit, not the "value-added" type. Frequent audits will keep a chief investment officer and staff on their toes and underscore the board's determination to prevent wrongdoing.

Fifth, consider prior relationships. The company should require investment managers, consultants, and other pension fund suppliers to disclose any prior relationship, business or otherwise, they might have had with anyone within the company. That is not to say prior relationships are unacceptable. Rather, the purpose of this information is to permit other decision makers the opportunity to ask the individual to remove himself or herself from decisions that might affect the pension fund's relationship with that supplier.

Finally, the company should ask the investment managers, consultants, and other pension fund suppliers to submit quarterly reports detailing any entertainment expenses they incurred on behalf of the pension fund staff, the chief investment officer, or anyone else involved with the pension fund. This list would include such things as business luncheons, tickets for sporting and other events, and any other entertainment. Again, this is not to imply that these activities are prohibited; the purpose is to allow the company to decide if the entertainment is becoming excessive and might be viewed as economic blackmail or bribery.

PREPARE, STRENGTHEN, AND ENFORCE A CODE OF ETHICS

Here is what one member of a company's board of directors said when asked why his company's pension fund did not have a code of ethics specifically for its pension fund investment personnel: "It's impossible to write a code of ethics or any such document that will cover every conceivable situation. [Our company] does have a corporate 'Code of Conduct' which I find adequate as an overall guideline for employee behavior."

To expect a "one size fits all," generic corporate code of ethics to apply to pension fund investments is foolhardy. The level of sophistication, the ability to easily cast wrongdoing as a judgment call, and the propensity of senior executives to avoid liability for lower level misdeeds, makes pension fund investments an entirely different ballgame than what the company is used to in its normal business activities.

Moreover, some actions may be perfectly acceptable under a generic code for the corporation, but inappropriate for the pension fund. For example, a company's generic code might allow an employee to spend corporate money or use corporate resources on charitable, political, or other noncorporate activities as long as he or she receives prior approval. On the other hand, even if a senior executive approves, it is against the law to use pension fund assets and resources for any reason other than in the interest of plan participants — no exceptions. Senior executives who are used to using corporate assets and resources may wrongly extend that attitude to the pension fund, assuming it's okay because they received prior approval.

Furthermore, consider this excerpt from the section of a company's generic code which deals with outside employment:

> Since each employee's primary obligation is to the company, any form of outside activity, including employment or self-employment, must be kept totally separate from employment with the company.

Under a strict reading of the company's generic code, it is acceptable for a senior executive of the pension fund's internal investment policy committee to accept a trustee position with a broker-sponsored mutual fund. After all, that outside employment is separate from his employment with the company. However, when viewed from the pension fund perspective, his part-time job can be considered a potential conflict of interest with the pension fund, especially if that broker does business with the pension fund.

Now consider this excerpt from a section of a company's generic code:

> If you leave the company, you must not use confidential business relationships, or other confidential information gained while in our employ, to compete with this company or its affiliates.

This paragraph would not prohibit a senior executive who was in a pension fund decision-making role from leaving the company and joining a consulting firm that did hundreds of thousands of dollars of business with the pension fund, or from joining an investment manager's firm just after allocating pension fund assets to that firm. Neither the consulting firm nor the investment management firm compete with the company or its affiliates.

The actions outlined above are not a violation of the cited sections of the company's generic code, might be perfectly acceptable to senior executives, might not violate any laws, and, indeed, may even be common business practices on the corporate side. But plan participants probably want those involved in the investment management of their pension fund's assets held to a higher standard. Instead of the generic sections, these might be more appropriate for pension fund personnel:

1. Any outside employment, with any firm that has done, or may even be likely to do, business with the pension fund, by any employee or director of the company who was in any way associated with the activities of the pension fund, regardless of their rank or position in the company, is prohibited.

2. As a condition of employment, employees associated with the pension fund agree they will not join the firm of an investment manager, consultant, or other supplier to the pension for a period of one year after they leave the employ of this company. As an alternative, the investment manager, consultant, or other supplier can choose to relinquish the pension fund account. If neither occurs, the pension fund will exercise its right to terminate the account relationship.

Prohibiting any type of part-time outside employment by anyone involved in pension fund investments stops many potential conflicts of interest. Prohibiting a pension fund employee from joining the firm of a pension fund supplier for at least one year removes one of the motivations for mutual backscratching.

Other ideas of what should be included in a pension fund code of ethics appear in Appendix 2 to this chapter.

The code of ethics should not be allowed to become a document someone simply files in a desk drawer. A way has to be found to get everyone, from secretaries to board members, involved in and thinking about ethics. An example would be to ask them to prepare an ethics statement they feel the pension fund should adopt, or, at the minimum, to list the areas they feel should be included in such a document. This task would force them to think about the issues. The lists can then be consolidated and redistributed to those individuals for review before the code is finalized.

But time passes, people forget, and new employees come on board. One way to keep the issues fresh in everyone's mind is to require each person to annually complete a questionnaire which addresses their compliance with the code. For example, the following question might be in the questionnaire:

> Q. Are you a director, officer, sole owner, partner, or employee of a consultant or advisor to any business enterprise that has supplied or is seeking to supply goods or services to the pension fund?

Yes _____   No _____

Having to check "yes" or "no" requires someone to read and to think about the question. That should keep a person involved and help underscore the standards the company is trying to maintain. Of course, lying on the questionnaire is cause for immediate dismissal.

Since much wrongdoing can be hidden from view, a chief investment officer and others in a decision-making role should be required to provide to a compliance officer (to be discussed later) a certified copy of his or her 1040 tax return, including a copy of Schedule D. Schedule D is that part of the tax return that deals with profits and losses from personal trading activity. Sure, someone could falsify the information so the real crooks might slip through, but requiring disclosure may help dissuade someone who is on the fence. At the minimum, this requirement to share specific tax information with the company's designated compliance officer sends a signal that the company is serious about ethics and about doing whatever it takes to ensure that high ethical standards in its pension fund are maintained. This request would be made of company employees.

Everyone in the company who is involved in pension fund investments should be made aware of the company's policies. But why stop there? The pension fund's investment managers, consultants, and other pension fund suppliers should also be made aware of the company's ethical expectations.

Most investment managers are reputable and will not knowingly engage in any unethical practices. But what constitutes unethical behavior? For example, most people would agree that setting up a slush fund, arranging discount purchases on cars, or kicking back cash to the chief investment officer for being awarded a pension fund account is unethical behavior. But how about providing a chief investment officer with money-making tips or taking clients and spouses out to a four-star restaurant? Are tickets to the Super Bowl OK if the investment manager accompanies the chief investment officer, but not OK if the chief investment officer initiates the request and just his or her friends attend?

Where is the line drawn? Each pension fund will have to decide that for itself, after seeking input from the lawyers, the consultants, the pension fund's staff members, and the plan's participants. However, once the code of ethics has been prepared and all those involved within the company are on board, the pension fund's suppliers should be informed of the company's ethical standards and should become involved in ensuring compliance. The most direct approach is to include statements about the company's ethical expectations in the investment manager's contract with the pension fund. Here are some examples of what could be included:

- The investment manager agrees that, as a condition of employment, he or she will adhere to the spirit and letter of the pension fund's code of ethics.

- Annually, the investment manager will provide the pension fund with a statement that he or she has complied with the company's code of ethics and, if necessary, provide an explanation of any deviations.
- The investment manager will submit quarterly reports to the company's designated compliance officer detailing entertainment expenses the investment manager incurred on behalf of the pension fund staff, chief investment officer, or anyone else involved with the pension fund up, through, and including the company's board of directors. This list would include such things as business luncheons, tickets for sporting and other events, and any other entertainment.

Including the company's expectations in the contract, with provisions for following up, lets the investment manager, consultant, and other pension fund suppliers know where the company has drawn the line. If they do not like the company's position, then they do not have to accept the account. It is as simple as that. This approach aligns the interests of pension fund suppliers, who want to keep the pension fund account, with those of a company, which wants to create and maintain a highly ethical environment.

Actually, a pension fund should start the ethical review even before a supplier is hired. For example, when a pension fund gets serious about hiring a firm, they should ask for the following information:

- A copy of the ethics statement or code of conduct which the supplier expects *their* employees to maintain.
- An itemized list of any finder fees or special incentive payments made in order to secure the pension fund's business.
- A list of any previous associations with anyone in the company — from secretaries to board members — and an explanation of the association.

It should be stressed with potential suppliers that there are no right or wrong answers to these questions. For example, prior associations with employees, especially pension fund personnel, are not necessarily bad. In fact, that may be a sign that a good working relationship has developed so that the supplier can "hit the ground running." Disclosure. That's what this is all about.

A copy of the company's code of ethics for its pension fund personnel should be included in the annual report to plan participants, as discussed in a previous section of this chapter. In addition, a letter personally signed by all company employees who are plan fiduciaries attesting that they lived up to the letter and spirit of the code should also be included in the annual report, so that they are on record.

APPOINT AN OMBUDSMAN AND A COMPLIANCE OFFICER

Some employees and pension fund suppliers may feel uncomfortable reporting wrongdoing by senior executives to senior management. To overcome this reluctance and provide the individual some anonymity, the company should appoint an ombudsman to whom pension fund employees and suppliers could talk if their boss or others at the company ask them to engage in an activity that smacks of impropriety. The ombudsman should be someone perceived to be of high integrity, who is outside the pension fund investment loop and has the clout to change things. Perhaps a senior member of the board of directors might play this role. In addition — not as a substitute — the company should establish a hotline to provide more immediate access to someone who can help a pension fund employee or supplier to sort out an ethical dilemma.

A compliance officer, who could be the same individual as the ombudsman or could even be an outside auditor, would (1) make sure the ethical statements are prepared, issued, and reviewed; (2) review the income tax returns for key pension fund decision makers; (3) be the contact point for pension fund supplier compliance; and (4) provide for ethics education for pension fund staff through and including the company's board of directors.

ESTABLISH PROPER OWNERSHIP OF PENSION ASSETS

Pension plan terminations, either initiated by the company's own management or as a result of a merger or acquisition, can cause hardship for plan participants. However, the issue of a company's right to terminate a plan is one thing; the ownership of the pension fund's assets is another.

We own the assets, say senior executives. They argue that, in a defined benefit plan, all the company ever promised plan participants was a monthly check at retirement, nothing more. How the company keeps that promise, if they do, is up to them. Senior executives, with a compliant board of directors, will decide how the pension assets are to be invested; what information beyond that required by law will be shared with plan participants; if and when the plan will be terminated; and, if the plan is terminated, how any "excess" assets will be distributed (subject to certain government restrictions).

Senior executives can be very practical about the ownership issue, however. Pension plan documents can contain a statement that, should there be a change in control of the company (such as an acquisition), the excess assets in the pension fund, if any, are to be used exclusively to provide retirement benefits. This puts the excess assets beyond the reach of an unwelcomed raider.

However, the door to the assets is still left open for senior executives. They still retain the right, as spelled out in the pension plan document, to terminate the plan and lay claim to any excess pension fund assets anytime *they* want. Moreover, they can get any barriers removed and pave the way for the outside raider to use the pension fund's excess assets any way they please. Most senior executives are conscientious and will do what's in the best interests of plan participants, but others might do what's in their own best interests.

Trustees should remove the issue of access to excess assets from the table. It should be clearly spelled out in the trust document that *all* the assets in the pension fund irrevocably belong to the plan participants and are beyond the reach of outside corporate raiders and senior executives alike.

APPENDIX 1

Pension Fund Annual Report

The following outline presents what the author thinks should be communicated to plan participants in an annual report. The annual report should include at least five years of historical data so that plan participants can identify trends.

I. **Asset allocation information.** At the minimum, this should include:
   A. A summary of the fund's asset allocation study, with a discussion of why a particular normal asset mix was selected.
   B. The pension fund's actual year-end asset mix, with an explanation of why management felt it was necessary to have the actual asset mix vary from the normal asset mix.

II. **Investment strategy information.** At the minimum, this should include:
   A. A copy of the investment strategy for each investment type and an explanation of why each was adopted.
   B. Year-end market value of the assets allocated to each investment type.

III. **Funded status.** At the minimum, this should include:
   A. The pension plan's liabilities, with an explanation of how they were estimated and the assumptions that were used.
   B. Year-end market value of the pension fund's total assets.
   C. The pension plan's funded status. If the plan is underfunded (assets are less than liabilities), what plans does the company have to correct the situation?
   D. Company contributions (if any).
   E. Benefit payments to retirees.
   F. Number and type of plan participants.

IV. Performance results. At the minimum, this should include:

    A. The pension fund's performance, with several benchmarks for comparison. The benchmarks should include peer group results, so that plan participants can see how their fund performed relative to other pension funds with similar objectives, and the normal asset mix weighted return (see Chapter 5), so that plan participants can see how their fund performed relative to the asset allocation study mix.

    B. The performance of the assets allocated to each investment type, with several benchmarks for comparison. The benchmarks should include the returns that would have been achieved if the assets were invested in index funds, so that plan participants can see how well the pension fund's investment strategy is working.

    C. The performance of each investment manager grouped by investment type, with several benchmarks for comparison. The benchmarks should include the composite return for each investment style, so that plan participants can see how well an individual manager is performing relative to the other investment managers with similar styles hired by the pension fund.

V. Expense information. At the minimum, this information should be grouped by categories such as investment manager fees, consulting fees, finder's fees, brokerage commissions, pension fund salaries, and operating expenses. Each category would further identify the supplier, the size of assets they manage for the pension fund, the fees they were paid, any finder's fees the supplier paid to get the account, whether the supplier was paid by soft dollar arrangements, the key person responsible for the pension fund's account, and a brief description of the services their firm rendered.

VI. Issues and policy. At the minimum, management should discuss these issues:

    A. Significant changes during the past year in the pension fund's asset mix, investment strategy, investment managers, consultants, and other pension fund suppliers, and the reasons for the changes.

    B. Significant changes in pension fund personnel or decision-making structure, and the reasons for the changes.

VII. Ethics-related information. At the minimum, this should include:

    A. A copy of the pension fund's code of conduct signed by the fiduciaries of the plan attesting that they have lived up to the letter and spirit of the code.

    B. A statement outlining any conflicts of interest or party-in-interest transactions, including dollar amounts and persons involved.

    C. A statement by the chief investment officer attesting to the fact that the investment managers, consultants, brokers, and other suppliers have been given a copy of the pension fund's code of conduct, and the pension fund has received written agreement from them that they will abide by its provisions.

VIII. Personnel-related information. At the minimum, this should include:

    A. Names, titles, and duties for every employee who is involved in the pension fund investment decision-making process, from the board of directors to senior investment personnel.

    B. Brief biographical summaries for all key pension fund decision makers within the company, including relevant members of the company's board of directors. The biographical summaries should also include all outside affiliations, jobs, and directorships.

IX. Signed actuarial report

X. Signed auditor's report

XI. Signed trustee's report

APPENDIX 2

Topics to Include in a Pension Fund Code of Ethics

- Conflicts of interest.
- Outside employment.
- Compliance with ERISA, the SEC, and other applicable rules and regulations.
- Insider trading and other security trading issues.
- Communicating inside information to others.
- Front running.
- Writing reports that support predetermined conclusions.
- Failure to use diligence and thoroughness in making recommendations.
- Misrepresenting performance.
- Misuse of proprietary, sensitive, or nonpublic information.
- Keeping inaccurate books and records.
- Abuse of expense accounts.
- Bribery.
- Kickbacks.
- Receiving excessive gifts and entertainment.
- Responsibilities of supervisors.
- Responsibilities of subordinates.
- Disclosure of additional compensation arrangements.
- Disclosure of referral fees.
- Discrimination and sexual harassment.
- Drug and alcohol abuse.
- Employee theft.

CHAPTER 11

The Role of Retirees

The sad truth is that, unlike shareowners (who can sell their shares if they are disgusted with senior management) or employees (who can always leave the company), pension plan participants are stuck. They can't leave the pension fund. They are locked in and are dependent upon whatever is dictated to them. Often, they do not have a voice in the affairs of the pension fund and are kept in the dark about what is going on. This is wrong.

Company employees who participate in the pension plan are in a difficult position. If they speak out, they run the risk of losing their jobs. This is why retirees must take the lead in time press for change. This chapter will outline what actions they can take.

AN ALLIANCE OF RETIREES

Shareowners select the company's board of directors, and the board, through its selection of the pension fund's investment committee members, determines who are the plan's trustees. So, ultimately, the shareowners control the trustees. If trustees aren't the instruments of change, action must be taken by shareowners to replace them.

It is virtually impossible for one person alone to get any action out of a company. Numbers are what count; that is why retirees need to form an alliance. They can send a message to the board of directors with the power their numbers, and, more importantly, the collective ownership their common stock gives them.

161

Retirees may not realize that, in aggregate, they own a lot of a company's stock. They may have gained this ownership position from years of discount purchases offered by many companies, from employee stock ownership plans, from dividend reinvestment programs, or, more recently, from participation in 401(k) "savings plans." And they are not alone. Other retirees from other companies might also own much of the company's stock, either directly or through mutual funds.

Stock ownership is power. This power is currently being dissipated by retirees who vote their shares along with the wishes of management either because they don't know what's really going on behind the scenes with their pension funds or they don't truly appreciate the power they have to control their own destiny.

However, others, primarily institutional shareowners, are using their power to influence corporate decisions:

> Heeding major shareowners' claims that "Joe has to go," Kmart Corp. forced embattled Joseph Antonini to relinquish his posts as president and chief executive officer, effective immediately . . . Kmart Chairman Donald Perkins cited unrelenting pressure from large institutional holders for the board's unanimous decision . . .[1]

But subsequent events put into motion, intentionally or unintentionally, by institutional shareowners may not be favorable to Kmart's pension plan participants. In fact, shortly after the change in management, Kmart announced it was stopping its contributions to its $1.4 billion pension plan.

Consider, too, this statement in reference to a chief executive officer's performance-based salary:

> "The dirty little secret is that institutional investors are just as greedy as everybody else," says Jon Lukomnik, deputy comptroller for pensions for New York City, whose five pension funds have assets of about $50 billion . . . Within reason, Mr. Lukomnik says, "we don't care how much you make [as the CEO] — as long as you make us a ton of money as well."[2]

That's fine for performance-seeking institutional investors, but will the push for performance-based salary eventually undercut the secu-

---

1. "Kmart's Embattled CEO Resigns Post Under Pressure from Key Shareholders," *The Wall Street Journal*, March 22, 1995.
2. "Raking It In," *The Wall Street Journal*, April 12, 1995.

rity of the pension promise as executives look for ways to reduce expenses, including pension expenses?

An alliance of plan participants, with retirees at the lead, will be heard in the boardroom. Forming such an alliance will not be easy, however. The first difficulty is assembling a database on fellow retirees. Some companies provide directories of retirees, others do not. The next problem is communication. A company's retirees may be scattered throughout the United States and perhaps even the world. Getting a message out could be difficult. Finally, there is the matter of expense. It costs money, lots of money, to send letters to every retiree. Postage, envelopes, and reproduction costs (assuming some retirees volunteer to address and stuff envelopes) could cost 50 cents a letter. For a company with thousands and thousands of retirees, just one mailing could cost tens of thousands of dollars. The company can afford this, but an individual retiree probably could not.

These are formidable, but not insurmountable, obstacles. First, if the company won't provide a list of retirees, an alternative is to place a small ad in a newspaper, such as the *AARP Bulletin*. The ad would ask retirees to join the alliance by providing their names, addresses, and the number of shares of the company's stock they own. Communication and cost barriers can be overcome by using a chain letter approach. A small group of retirees starts it by sending letters to their retired friends, requesting them to send copies to their retired friends, and so forth. Once the chain is established, it can be quite effective. An alternative means of communication, which is becoming increasingly viable, is to use the electronic bulletin boards set up by various networks such as the Internet, America On-line, and Prodigy. If a retiree doesn't have access to these networks, perhaps a relative or friend does; even a retiree's public library might provide the service.

To reiterate, the collective shares of the alliance could represent a significant ownership position, which, when voted as a block, could have a major impact on the direction the company takes with respect to the pension promise.

Representation on the Board of Directors

Once an alliance is formed, the first thing it should focus on is getting one of its own elected to the company's board of directors. Retirees must have someone who represents their interests in the boardroom when the door closes. Being there won't automatically prevent misguided policies by the majority, but at least retirees will have access to detailed pension fund information and a bully pulpit to rally other retirees into action. Make no mistake: Decisions made by the board of directors and senior executives can have a direct, material impact on the lives of retirees. To repeat, it is *essential* that retirees get one of their own on the company's board of directors.

It won't be easy, however. First, it means mobilizing retirees to back a single candidate — their candidate — for board membership. Who should that person be is not an easy decision. The candidate needs to have experience but also be independent from senior executive influence.

Once a candidate is selected, the next step is to get that person elected. The hurtles here are daunting indeed. There is a maze of government rules and corporate regulations and expense to go through. Consider the following:

> Under current rules, companies are only required to send shareholders a proxy statement and ballot card with names of the companies' nominees. Shareholders who want to recommend other candidates must send out separate proxies and ballot cards at their own expense.[3]

Changes in corporate election rules are long overdue, and retirees should press their lawmakers to do whatever is necessary to achieve true shareowner democracy. But that's a long-term goal; right now, an alliance would have to use its persuasive powers with current board members and with management so that when an open spot becomes available an alliance choice is named. Absent that, the alliance is forced to go through the election hoops.

Shareowner Proposals

Another approach to getting some specific provisions acted upon by the company, such as a requirement that the company provide plan participants with a readable and relevant pension fund annual report, is to get a shareowner proposal into the company's proxy statement.

---

3. "Investor Rights Considered," *Pension & Investments*, May 3, 1993.

That proposal would then come up for a vote at the company's next annual meeting, and alliance members would have the opportunity to support it. If trustees drag their feet on implementing change, this is one way to force action.

The advantages of getting a shareowner proposal into the proxy material are communication and cost savings. The company would send out the proxy statement to all shareowners, so the company would bear the burden of the cost of communication. The difficulties, however, are mind-boggling. First, shareowner proposals typically can be submitted only once a year. If a retiree fails to get the proposal into the current proxy statement, he or she may have to wait a full year to try again. Second, there are numerous limitations on what can be included in the proxy material. Finally, a labyrinth of rules and regulations surrounds shareowner proposals (see Appendix 1 to this chapter, which reproduces a section from the Security and Exchange Commission rules). There is ample opportunity for the company's high-priced lawyers to block a shareowner's proposal from coming to a vote.

Here are some of the documents an individual might find useful when he or she tries to get a shareowner proposal into the company's proxy material. From the company, obtain copies of (1) the by-laws of the corporation; (2) the company's Certificate of Incorporation; and (3) the latest proxy statement. From the Security and Exchange Commission (Washington, D.C. 20549), obtain copies of (1) Proxy Rules, Regulation 14A — Solicitation of Proxies; (2) Schedule 14A; and (3) Release No. 34-31326.

Be forewarned — there is an absolute maze of regulations and legalese. An attorney *might* help, but given the way the regulations are written, the deck is stacked in favor of the company.

Other shareowners might feel threatened by retiree alliances or retiree proposals appearing in the proxy statements. They shouldn't be. Nothing suggested here would interfere with the management of the business of the company. The only thing being addressed is the need to make sure the pension promise is secure. Proper funding and the investment management of a pension fund that has adequate controls to frustrate wrongdoers is in the long-run interest of all shareowners.

Securities and Exchange Commission Proxy Rule 14a–8c

The registrant may omit a proposal and any statement in support thereof from its proxy statement and form of proxy under any of the following circumstances:

1. If the proposal is, under the law of the restraint's domicile, not a proper subject for action by security holders.

   Note: Whether a proposal is a proper subject for action by security holders will depend on the applicable state law. Under certain states' laws, a proposal that mandates certain action by the registrant's board of directors may not be a proper subject matter for shareholder action, while a proposal recommending or requesting such action of the board may be proper under such state laws.

2. If the proposal, if implemented, would require the registrant to violate any state law or Federal law of the United States, or any law of any foreign jurisdiction to which the registrant is subject, except that this provision shall not apply with respect to any foreign law compliance with which would be violative of any state law or Federal law of the United States.

3. If the proposal or the supporting statement is contrary to any of the Commission's proxy rules and regulations, including Rules 14a–9, which prohibits false or misleading statements in proxy soliciting materials.

4. If the proposal relates to the redress of a personal claim or grievance against the registrant or any other person, or if it is designed to result in a benefit to the proponent or to further a personal interest, which benefit or interest is not shared with the other security holders at large.

5. If the proposal relates to operations which account for less than 5 percent of the registrant's total assets at the end of its most recent fiscal year, and for less than 5 percent of its net earnings and gross sales for its most recent fiscal year,

and is not otherwise significantly related to the registrant's business.

6. If the proposal deals with a matter beyond the registrant's power to effectuate.

7. If the proposal deals with a matter relating to the conduct of the ordinary business operations of the registrant.

8. If the proposal relates to an election to office.

9. If the proposal is counter to a proposal to be submitted by the registrant at the meeting.

10. If the proposal has been rendered moot.

11. If the proposal is substantially duplicative of a proposal previously submitted to the registrant by another proponent, which proposal will be included in the registrant's proxy material for the meeting.

12. If the proposal deals with substantially the same subject matter as a prior proposal submitted to security holders in the registrant's proxy statement and form of proxy relating to any annual or special meeting of security holders held within the preceding five calendar years, it may be omitted from the registrant's proxy materials relating to any meeting of security holders held within three calendar years after the last such previous submission: Provided, that:

    (i) If the proposal was submitted at only one meeting during such preceding period, it received less than three percent of the total number of votes cast in regard thereto; or

    (ii) If the proposal was submitted at only two meetings during such preceding period, it received at the time of its second submission less than six percent of the total number of votes cast in regard thereto; or

    (iii) If the prior proposal was submitted at three or more meetings during such preceding period, it received at the time of its last submission less than 10 percent of the total number of votes cast in regard thereto; or

13. If the proposal relates to specific amounts of cash or stock dividends.

CHAPTER 12

The Proper Role
of Government

We ask the government to solve our problems; what we get is bureaucracy, unintelligible regulations, higher taxes, and so on. Is that what we want? Of course not. Nevertheless, the fact remains that there are some things for which we must look to the government for help — and its involvement doesn't have to mean increased bureaucracy or higher costs.

This chapter will outline the actions trustees and retirees should press our lawmakers to take in order to help protect a pension fund from wrongdoing by company employees.

HELP HONEST PENSION FUND EMPLOYEES

Many pension fund employees are aware of at least some of the questionable activities initiated by self-serving senior executives, but fear of retaliation prevents them from coming forward. Under the laws in some states they are considered "employees-at-will," which means that they can be fired with or without cause anytime senior management chooses. Point the finger upward and you risk it being broken off.

The government must level the playing field. First, lawmakers need to remove the negative legal incentives preventing these employees from coming forward, then provide positive incentives for them to report wrongdoing.

One of the first negative incentives that must be neutralized is the "employment-at-will" doctrine. The most effective approach is to expand the antiretaliation section of ERISA to provide protection for pension fund employees who report wrongdoing to the company's senior executives. In addition, lawmakers should provide for stiff penalties to be imposed on any company or senior executive who violates this extended protection, and, even further, they should provide the legal basis for the injured party to seek significant punitive damages for a company's or individual's egregious retaliatory behavior. A company would still have many retaliation weapons left in its arsenal, but at least negating any state "employment-at-will" doctrines via changes in ERISA means there is one less legal barrier for an honest employee to overcome.

However, leveling the playing field is not enough. We must demand that our lawmakers tilt the balance in favor of honest pension fund employees who report wrongdoing. We need to put ethics on the offensive by providing positive incentives for an employee to come forward and, in the process, an incentive for companies to get serious about the ethical environment in their pension funds. We urgently need to press our lawmakers to extend the so-called "Lincoln Law" to pension fund employees.

The "Lincoln Law" was enacted in 1863 to help fight fraud in the provision of Union troops during the Civil War (hence its name). Apparently, suppliers were defrauding the government by providing shoddy goods to the military. This law provided whistle-blowers with government protection. Over 100 years later, in 1986, the law was liberalized and retitled the False Claims Act. Basically, the law

> permits a private party to file suit on behalf of the U.S. against anyone who has made false claims with the government. Federal officials have the option of taking over the cases, but whistle-blowers are entitled to 15% to 30% of any recovery, plus attorney's fees.[1]

This law has been successful in combating defense contractor fraud and, more recently, health care fraud:

> Since 1986, about 516 suits have been brought, with total recoveries of about $358 million . . .[2]

---

1. "Whistles Blow More Often on Health Care," *The Wall Street Journal*, September 2, 1993.
2. Ibid.

This is a wonderful arrangement, which should be extended to the pension fund environment. It would put hundreds of people on the alert for wrongdoing and fraud within the companies to which it applies. These are employees who know what's going on, know why it's going on, know who is involved, and have the proof to back up their claims. Activities that once could be easily hidden from an outside investigator can now be exposed from within the company. In one fell swoop, the law would release knowledgeable "auditors" within the company to ensure that plan participants are not getting cheated. The mere fact that such oversight exists should dampen senior executives' appetite for wrongdoing.

The author proposes that, if a pension fund employee sees wrongdoing in a pension fund, he or she would be able to sue on behalf of the plan participants, and federal officials in the Pension and Welfare Benefits Administration (PWBA) would have the option of taking over the case. If the case is successful, the whistle-blower would be entitled to 15 to 30 percent of any recovery plus attorney's fees. The bounty should also be extended to the local PWBA office. That is, the local office would also be entitled to 15 to 30 percent of any recovery, which would then be required to go into a bonus pool for staff personnel in that office. The end result is if senior management was proven to have their hands in the pension fund cookie jar, the company would have to fully reimburse the pension fund and pay 15 to 30 percent to the whistle-blower and another 15 to 30 percent to the local PWBA office. Talk about an effective deterrent to wrongdoing!

Not surprisingly, some have called the False Claims Act a "bounty-hunting law" and question its "mercenary" nature. In the author's opinion, if the law is set up in a fair manner, and the company or individual is proven guilty, more power to the whistle-blower in exposing wrongdoing. The whistle-blower provides a useful service to society by exposing wrongdoing and fraud that heretofore had been concealed. To overcome objections that this extension to the pension fund environment would invite frivolous litigation, perhaps some fixed dollar amount could be put into the law that would have to be paid to the company by the person who brought the suit if that individual was unable to prove his or her case. This would deter frivolous suits.

Appropriate protection and incentives for whistle-blowers assure participants that senior executives will look out for their interests, because it will be clearly in the company's own best interest to do so.

ELIMINATE SECTION 415 LIMITATIONS

Government-sponsored Section 415 limitation policies are misguided. As described in Chapter 3, Section 415 limitations are the government's attempt to block senior executives from receiving what the government considers overly generous retirement income at the taxpayer's expense by limiting the amount of money that can be paid out of the pension fund to any given retiree.

The government has been continually squeezing downward the amounts that can be paid from the pension fund. This has two serious consequences for pension plan participants. First, with the wave of downsizing in corporate America, many lower- to middle-level management employees who were compelled or forced into early retirement are finding that a portion of their retirement income is now coming from unsecured supplemental plans, not from the pension fund. It should surprise no one that senior executives, who were the alleged targets of the Section 415 limitations, have protected themselves with other trust funds and insurance policies. Lower- to middle-level employees, now retirees, have no such protection. They are at increased risk of seeing a portion — in some cases over half — of their retirement income getting wiped out. This is turning the clock back to pre-ERISA days, when retirees were at great risk of losing their retirement incomes should anything happen to the company.

The second consequence of the government's constant squeezing downward of the amount that can be paid from the pension fund is that it is undermining the security of the pension fund itself. They are doing this by reducing the amount of personal stake a senior executive has in the pension fund's financial well-being. The gradual elimination of a senior executive's personal stake in the pension fund, coupled with the increase in the popularity of corporate earnings-based compensation packages, means that when push comes to shove in the boardroom senior executives will opt for increasing corporate earnings rather than increasing retiree security. It is possible that senior executives will fiddle with pension fund assumptions and/or increase the risk of the pension fund's investments in order to paper over any shortfalls in the pension fund. But this can last only so long before the facade comes tumbling down, and by that time, the short-term results motivated senior management team will be long gone, leaving another team and possibly the government — and ultimately the taxpayers — to pick up the pieces.

Ways are needed to increase — not reduce — a senior executive's reliance on the pension fund for his or her retirement well-being. Self-interest is a strong motivator, and making senior executives dependent on the financial soundness of the pension fund seems to be a cost-effective way to make sure the pension fund is free from wrongdoing.

Section 415 should be abolished, and all pension payments (regular and supplemental) should be paid out of the pension fund and be tax deductible for the company. Any loss in government tax revenue can be made up with an increase in taxes on executive stock option incentive plans — but not so much as to kill the incentive plans as a way of motivating senior executives. These two actions — eliminating Section 415 and increasing the taxes on stock option incentive plans — would help focus senior executive attention on making sure the pension fund is financially sound, well-managed, and free from wrongdoing while under their stewardship, because it would be in their own personal interests to make it so. This might also help senior executives to focus more on long-term results rather than the quarter-to-quarter expediencies that seem to plague some American corporations.

Finally, senior executives should be barred from taking a lump-sum distribution from their pension fund. Perhaps this can be accomplished by setting a low dollar limit on the lump-sum amount that can be taken out of a pension fund without a severe federal tax impact. This would make it far less attractive for senior executives to withdraw the funds accumulated on their behalf. At least a portion of their retirement well-being would be tied to the financial well-being of their company's pension fund. Retired senior executives then would have an incentive to do whatever they can to ensure that those who follow them in the company will maintain the safety and security of the pension fund.

STANDARDIZE PLAN ASSUMPTIONS AND COMPEL COMPANIES TO FULLY FUND PENSION PLANS WITHOUT REDUCING BENEFITS

Using wildly different mortality and investment earnings assumptions stretches credibility. Sure, there are differences between companies, industries, and regions of the country, but it is difficult to imagine they are as large as some of the differences in pension plan liability assumptions suggest. Because these assumptions are so important in determining whether a plan is fully funded or grossly underfunded, tighter guidelines are necessary, no matter how much we may dislike government intervention.

Some action has been taken to help out the PBGC. Buried in the General Agreement on Tariffs and Trade Agreement (GATT), which was signed into law in early December 1994, were provisions which, among other things, will accelerate the funding requirements for pension plans that are underfunded and increase insurance premiums. Labor Secretary Robert Reich, chairman of the PBGC's board, said the new regulations are expected to cut underfunding by more than two-thirds over the next 15 years.[3] Mr. Martin Slate, Executive Director of the PBGC, was reported to have said: "Strengthening pensions through better funding will strengthen the system as a whole . . . Workers and companies can now have greater confidence in a stronger pension system and the PBGC."[4]

These are fine efforts, but they don't go far enough, fast enough. Some provisions allow companies to stretch the implemention of changes over a decade. Consider this: It was reported that the mortality table in the bill, a 10-year-old, 1983 version, can be more lenient than what some companies currently use. Moreover, the spread of permissible investment rate assumptions is still very large, and a company can always let the plan slip into 90 percent funded status. True, if it drops below 90 percent additional payments are required, but those payments can be spread out over as long as 13 years.

In addition, plan participants get short-changed. The bill uses the retirement system to help pay for GATT:

> To help offset the revenue losses from the reduction in tariffs under the General Agreement of Tariffs and Trade, the amounts U.S. employees can contribute to [defined contribution plans] will be scaled back, *and many workers will receive smaller pensions.*[5] [Emphasis added.]

---

3. "Underfunding of Pension Plans Widened in 1993," *The Wall Street Journal*, December 14, 1994.
4. "GATT Reworks Pensions," *Pension & Investments*, December 12, 1994.
5. "GATT Law to Squeeze U.S. Pensions," *The Wall Street Journal*, December 5, 1994.

How much smaller pensions?

Marjorie Martin, a vice president of Sedgwick Noble Lowndes, a Philadelphia benefits-consulting firm, says the GATT-required rate would mean a reduction of about 7% in the size of a lump-sum pension distribution for a 65-year-old employee.

Younger employees would face much larger reductions, she figures. A 55-year-old employee who took early retirement or simply switched jobs would get about 25% less under the GATT legislation, Ms. Martin says; a 45-year-old, she says would take a 50% cut, compared with rules in effect up to now.[6]

Aren't there laws against this type of thing? Well in this case the anticutback rules of ERISA were waived[7] — that's right, waived.

How much could come out of the pockets of future retirees? Mr. Slate estimates the provisions in GATT will raise $1 billion for the Treasury over five years.[8] It really should come as no surprise that the government wants to get its hands on every source of revenue it can.

The corporate lobbying effort was successful as well:

Companies with overfunded plans, such as AT&T Corp. and International Business Machines Corp., seized the chance to make hay of their own: They persuaded lawmakers to extend a pension-law provision, about to expire, that let them use excess funds to pay retiree medical expenses. DuPont Co., for example, will be able to keep using as much as $150 million a year of pension surpluses this way.[9]

Furthermore, an initial provision in the bill required companies that had pension plans that were underfunded by $50 million or more to notify the PBGC if they intended to merge with another company. The PBGC could then oppose deals where pension commitments were abandoned:

Employers began [the meeting with government officials] with an ultimatum. Michael Gulotta, a senior actuary at an AT&T unit, said employers would "absolutely not negotiate" the issue of allowing PBGC intrusion into mergers and acquisitions.[10]

6. "Pension Cutbacks in GATT legislation Scare Pre-Retirees and Bewilder Experts," *The Wall Street Journal*, December 13, 1994.
7. "GATT Law to Squeeze U.S. Pensions," *The Wall Street Journal*, December 5, 1994.
8. "GATT Reworks Pensions," *Pension & Investments*, December 12, 1994.
9. "Stealth Legislation — Pension Rules Tacked Quietly on Trade Bill Portend Vast Changes," *The Wall Street Journal*, March 15, 1995.
10. Ibid.

The notification provision was defeated for publicly held companies, but not for those privately held: "There were no private companies in the room" to defend themselves, a government negotiator notes.[11]

What should be galling to pension plan participants is that changes to the pension systems in this country were tacked onto a bill to liberalize world trade:

> "I was the last person in the world who would have thought GATT affected pension funds," says a 59-year-old librarian for a St. Louis chemical company, who declines to be named. She retired last December rather than wait until June, as planned, because she figured the bill could cost her $25,000 in benefits.[12]

REQUIRE COMPANIES TO PRODUCE ANNUAL REPORTS AND USE THEM TO REINFORCE THE ETHICS STATEMENT

Chapter 10 called on the pension fund's trustees to take certain actions, some of which may be difficult for them to institute. One critical action is the production of a relevant, readable annual report outlining the pension fund's investment activities and results.

The information a company is currently required by the government to provide in the Form 5500 Report is useless for most plan participants. Recently, the Department of Labor asked for comments on improving pension plan disclosure. The author submitted the detail provided in Appendix 2 of Chapter 10. It is not clear what, if anything, will result from this agency's efforts. Corporate lobby groups want less, not more, disclosure. Lawmakers need to get involved to reinforce the Department of Labor's efforts.

In addition to demanding more disclosure of pension fund activities, the lawmakers can use the opportunity to add teeth to an ethics statement:

> The threat of government sanctions and moral/religious beliefs are significantly more important deterrents to unethical behavior than are self-regulatory sanctions or published codes of ethics.[13]

---

11. Ibid.
12. Ibid.
13. "Ethics in the Investment Profession: A Survey," Research Foundation of the Institute of Chartered Financial Analysts, May 1992.

The annual report could be required to contain the company's pension fund ethics statement. This statement would be signed by all of the company's pension plan fiduciaries attesting to the fact that they have lived up to its provisions. Such a statement would get senior management's attention, especially if there were stiff penalties for falsification.

ELIMINATE HIDDEN TAXES

Finally, like mosquitoes on a summer night, government-initiated proposals will try to take a little bite out of a plan participant's retirement pocketbook:

> Every year pension plans show up on the Congressional Budget Office's list of tax benefits that might be eliminated to help close the budget deficit. The implication is that ending these tax benefits would be a costless way of reducing the deficit.[14]

A number of proposals have been tossed around. One suggested imposing a one-time tax of 15 percent on pension fund assets and thereafter annually taxing the pension fund's income. This proposal was expected to generate a whopping $450 billion in the first year and $50 billion a year thereafter!

A frontal assault on your retirement security by the tax authorities is too obvious and politically risky. A less obvious, more subtle way is for the government to encourage "social" investing. This could involve investing in highways, bridges, housing developments, and so forth. The buzzword in the industry for these types of expenditures is "economically targeted investments," or ETIs:

> Aren't pension funds supposed to be for the benefit of workers and retirees? Yes. Has that principle kept government away? No. A few states and localities, such as Massachusetts and New York City, have already begun directing a portion of state employees' investments to such investments as low-income housing. One of those funds, the Kansas Public Employees Retirement System, lost more than $100 million on socially targeted investments in the 1980s.[15]

---

14. "Evidence of Saving," editorial, *Pension & Investments*, April 5, 1993.
15. "Pensions Ripe for Democrats' Plucking," letter to the editor, *The Wall Street Journal*, August 19, 1993, Mr. Price.

> In his search for funds, [President] Clinton is casting a hungry eye
> on the world's biggest pool of money: $4 trillion worth of pension as-
> sets. At least three Cabinet chiefs — Robert B. Reich of Labor,
> Henry G. Cisneros of Housing & Urban Development, and Federico
> Pena of Transportation — have urged pension fund managers to tar-
> get some of their investments toward public needs.[16]
>
> Assistant Secretary of Labor Olena Berg has set the foundation for
> the Labor Department to create its first economically targeted invest-
> ment [ETI] clearinghouse . . . "We believe the existence of an ETI
> clearinghouse will heighten interest by both public and private (pen-
> sion) plans in ETI programs."[17]

New highways, bridge repairs, new housing are all important to
the general welfare of our country. But who decides what is socially
desirable? A government agency? The squeaky wheel? How are expected returns computed? What are the risks relative to the returns as
compared to other investments? Finally, and most importantly, will
pension funds be more secure after these investments are made?

If the government really wants these socially desirable investments, let's put them into some sort of "Great Society" program and
vote on the tax increases to pay for them, and not try to pick the pensioner's pocket through their pension fund.

Lest the reader think only one political party covets the pension
fund riches, the latest proposal (at least at this writing) was raised by
the Republican chairman of the House Ways and Means Committee.
According to newspaper reports, his plan would eliminate all restrictions on the use of the pension fund's excess assets, "excess" meaning
any amount greater than 125 percent of the plan's current liabilities.

> The bill would set up a window in which firms with excess pension
> assets could take them out of the plan free of a 6.5% excise tax. That
> tax would be imposed on transfers made after July 1, 1996. On top of
> the excise tax, assets transferred would be treated as business
> income.[18]

Aides to the committee estimated these changes would add
about $10 billion to the federal coffers over seven years. This, in turn,

---

16. "Uncle Sam Wants to Fix Potholes with Your Pension Fund," *Business Week*, May 3, 1993.
17. "ETI Clearinghouse Building Blocks Laid," *Pension & Investments*, March 7, 1994.
18. "Archer Plan Could Unlock $220 Billion in Pension Assets," *Investor's Business Daily*, Sep-
    tember 18, 1995.

would help balance the budget. Assistant Secretary of Labor, Olena Berg, referred to earlier as favoring a clearinghouse for economically targeted investments, was reported as saying: "This is truly a raid on pension plans."

The simple fact is that both political parties are looking to use the assets in your corporate pension funds to further their own objectives. Like it or not, your future financial security is being shaped by today's political decision makers. The only reasonable chance of stopping them is to use your vote and your voice. A clear message must be sent to your representatives to strengthen, not weaken, our corporate pension funds.

CHAPTER 13

In Summary

A lot of material has been covered in this book therefore a brief recap of the underlying realities and recommended changes taken might be helpful.

UNDERLYING REALITIES

This is the situation as it exists today in the pension fund industry:

1. The new culture of the disposable employee has diminished loyalties and trust within corporations. This harsher business environment can create an atmosphere where fraud and wrongdoing might flourish.

2. Pension fund investment management, consulting, and trading financial instruments are lucrative businesses. There are thousands of firms scrambling for a piece of the action. This creates opportunities for self-serving employees to exploit for their own personal advantage.

3. Conscientious trustees and senior executives who lack pension fund investment street smarts might be easily lulled into a false sense of security by clever employees.

4. Senior executives can retaliate against whistle-blowing pension fund employees with relative impunity; knowing this, people will think twice before reporting wrongdoing.

5. New executive compensation packages at many companies could focus senior management's attention on increasing corporate earnings at the expense of the company's pension promise.

6. Some senior executives might believe the pension fund's assets really belong to the company, not to plan participants, and therefore can be used to advance corporate goals.

7. Plan participants are not entitled to any information about their pension fund other than what is required by law — information which is meaningless and incomprehensible to most individuals.

8. "Golden parachutes" may encourage senior executives to proceed with mergers and acquisitions that have a negative impact on the pension promise but result in a huge financial windfall for themselves.

9. If a company is committed to protecting its senior executives, it has the money and legal power to frustrate the most diligent of investigators. It is difficult to detect wrongdoing in a pension fund from the outside looking in.

RECOMMENDED CHANGES

Below are the changes that should be taken by the trustees as the leading agents of change. If the trustees balk, then retirees must press for change — either directly with the trustees or with their lawmakers:

1. Negative incentives that block honest pension fund employees from reporting wrongdoing must be removed. At the minimum, the antiretaliation section of ERISA should be expanded to provide protection to employees who report wrongdoing to company senior executives.

2. Concurrent with the removal of negative incentives, the so-called "Lincoln Law" needs to be expanded to cover pension fund employees who report wrongdoing by senior executives. This extension would create a positive incentive for both the employee to report wrongdoing and the senior executives to avoid it.

3. Section 415 of the federal tax code should be abolished, with all retirement checks being paid from the pension fund. This would more closely align the interests of senior executives with those of the plan participants.

4. Companies should use standardized, conservative interest rate assumptions and mortality tables, and be required to keep their pension plans fully funded.

5. The company's pension fund decision-making organization needs to be streamlined and focused. All the bureaucracy and multiple reporting levels should be eliminated, and the chief investment officer and pension fund staff should report directly to the committee of the board of directors. Ideally that committee should be chaired by a retiree.

6. There is absolutely no excuse — repeat, no excuse — for less than full disclosure of pension fund investments, policies, strategies, and performance results. Currently, the information required by ERISA is incomplete and incomprehensible to most plan participants. A detailed, readable annual report should be made available to all plan participants.

7. Trustees need to use some common sense in auditing the pension fund. Simply relying on the chief investment officer to select the auditor and monitor the depth of the audit is naive at best, a breach of fiduciary responsibility at worst.

8. The company needs to develop a code of ethics exclusively for pension fund related personnel. The code of ethics should apply to *everyone* involved in pension fund investments, from secretaries to the board of directors. Moreover, pension fund suppliers should be made aware of the company's code and required to abide by it.

9. Companies should be required to include a copy of their code of ethics in their annual reports to plan participants. All of the company's pension fund fiduciaries should be required to sign a statement attesting that they have personally lived up to its provisions.

10. The company should appoint an ombudsman to whom honest employees can report questionable activities in complete confidence. A compliance officer should also be appointed to handle on-going ethical oversight.

11. Retirees must band together in an alliance in order to speak to boards of directors and senior executives with the power their numbers and collective ownership of common stock give them.

12. Finally, a way must be found to make it absolutely clear that the assets in the pension fund — all the assets — belong to the plan participants. This would put the assets beyond the reach of outside corporate raiders and inside company executives alike.

The author sincerely believes most individuals involved in pension fund investments are honest and conscientious. They want to do the right thing and would welcome the changes recommended in this book. No one should think, however, that just because a pension fund was safe in the past it will be secure in the future. The underlying realities are simply too strong to be ignored. A little of that old-fashioned "ounce of prevention" our mothers told us about is now called for. For once, let's correct a situation before it becomes a disaster.

INDEX

A

Access to information, 31–31
Actuary, 68
Annual report, 156–158, 176–177
Antonini, Joseph, 162
Asset mix
    defined, 35–38
    normal mix, 35
    ranges, 38
Asset ownership established, 154–155
Audits, pension fund, 146–149
    experience, 148
    guidelines, 148
    by independent organization, 148
    and internal auditing staff, 146–147
    prior relationships, 148
    quarterly reports, 148–149

B

Berg, Olena, 178, 179
Board of directors, 57–62
Boesky, Ivan, 1
Bolduc, J. P., 85

C

Cash kickbacks, 87–91
    indirect, 89–91
Chicanery, disclosing, 131–140
    chief investment officer involvement, 133–134
    collateral benefits, 131
    cover-up, 137–140
    fear of retaliation, 134–137
    senior management involvement, 133
Chief investment officer, 65
    involvement in chicanery, 133–134
    perks of the job, 91–94
    source of jobs, 97
    temptation, 83–84

O

P